THE
FORGIVING
CHRIST

THE FORGIVING CHRIST

A Book of Penitential Celebrations

William J. Freburger
James E. Haas

AVE MARIA PRESS   Notre Dame, Indiana 46556

THE AUTHORS

William J. Freburger, formerly Director of Liturgy for the Archdiocese of Baltimore, has long been active in diocesan and national liturgical affairs, and is associated with Time Consultants, Severna Park, Maryland. His many published works include *Repent and Believe* (1972), *This Is the Word of the Lord* (1974), and *Eucharistic Prayers for Children* (1976), co-authored with James Haas.

James E. Haas, a former Director of Religious Education at St. Joseph's parish in Fullerton, Maryland, is Director of Programming for Time Consultants, an advisor to the Bishops' Committee on the Liturgy, lecturer, composer and author of children's liturgy books and filmstrips. His books include: *Shout Hooray* (1972), *Make a Joyful Noise* (1973), *Praise the Lord* (1974), and *Eucharistic Prayers for Children* (1976).

Acknowledgments:

English translation of an excerpt from the Rite of Baptism for Children, excerpts from the Roman Missal, excerpts from Holy Communion and Worship of the Eucharist Outside Mass, excerpts from the Rite of Penance, Appendices II and III. Copyright © 1969, 1973, 1974, 1975, International Committee on English in the Liturgy, Inc. All rights reserved.

Nihil Obstat:
    Msgr. Carroll J. Satterfield, S.T.D.

Imprimatur:
    Most Rev. William D. Borders, D.D.

Library of Congress Catalog Card Number: 76-50442
International Standard Book Number: 0-87793-125-9

Art by Tom Hojnacki

Printed in the United States of America

Contents

Introduction

The revised *Rite of Penance* must be used in all dioceses of the United States after Lent of 1977. The official ritual is a pastoral handbook which should not be neglected. It is a rich treasury of inspiration and texts for the sacrament of Penance. However, in this book we are concentrating on only two of the more promising pastoral arrangements which the new Rite provides for our consideration: the communal celebration of the sacrament and the nonsacramental penitential celebrations.

Even before the introduction of the new *Rite of Penance*, communal celebrations of the sacrament had made their appearance on the pastoral-liturgical scene, and proved increasingly popular in diverse situations around the country. Immediately after the Second Vatican Council, as we awaited the reform of the ritual of Penance, these celebrations allowed parish communities to honor the liturgical principle enunciated by the Council: that the sacraments are sacraments of the Church and their celebration in common is to be preferred to a celebration by an individual, in a quasi-private manner (cf. *Constitution on the Sacred Liturgy,* nos. 26-27). In the 60s, these communal celebrations brought a variety unavailable in the unreformed ritual and introduced in striking fashion the ecclesial dimension of this particular sacrament in those situations, before Easter and Christmas, when large numbers of people traditionally present themselves for the celebration of Penance.

7

The new Rite now makes these celebrations a part of the official ritual for the sacrament. What originated in local initiative is now recognized as universal practice. "When a number of penitents assemble at the same time to receive sacramental reconciliation," says the Introduction to the Rite, "it is fitting that they be prepared for the sacrament by a celebration of the word of God" (no. 22). The text then gives a brief outline:

> The faithful listen together to the word of God, which proclaims his mercy and invites them to conversion; at the same time they examine the conformity of their lives with that word of God and help each other through common prayer. After each person has confessed his sins and received absolution, all praise God together for his wonderful deeds on behalf of the people he has gained for himself through the blood of his Son (ibid.).

The structure of the Liturgy of the Word which has become familiar to us during the past decade of liturgical reform has been applied here in the revision of the sacrament of Penance. The traditional format (one priest, one penitent) has now been enriched with this second form, communal in nature. The text of the ritual uses a somewhat cumbersome title to describe the celebration: "Rite for the Reconciliation of Several Penitents with Individual Confession and Absolution." The complete structure as presented by the Rite is as follows:

INTRODUCTORY RITES
    Song
    Greeting
    Introduction
    Opening Prayer
LITURGY OF THE WORD
    Reading
    Psalm (or song, or silence)
    Reading
    Gospel acclamation

Gospel
Homily
Examination of Conscience

RITE OF RECONCILIATION
General confession of sinfulness
Litany (or song)
Our Father
Individual confessions and absolution
Expression of praise (psalm, song, etc.)
Closing Prayer

CONCLUSION
Blessing
Dismissal

Within this general framework there are, of course, many possibilities for adaptation and options. For instance, in the Liturgy of the Word, there may be as many as three readings or as few as one (in which case, it would be the Gospel).

In addition to these sacramental celebrations in common, the ritual recommends the creative, pastoral use of non-sacramental penitential celebrations, "gatherings of the people of God to hear the proclamation of God's word" which "invites them to conversion and renewal of life and announces our freedom from sin through the death and resurrection of Christ" *(Rite of Penance,* no. 36). With the obvious caveat that these celebrations must not be confused with the sacrament of Penance, the ritual goes on to point out that such services can be helpful in creating a penitential consciousness and sustaining a spirit of conversion in the community.

In composing the celebrations contained in the body of this book, we had three purposes in mind. First, we constructed them in such a way that they may be used with or without the sacrament of Penance. Second, we have tried to be helpful by giving you a sufficient amount of resources, but we have not spelled out every last detail. Even with the amount of material which we offer here, you will still have to plan and prepare your community's version of our suggestion. Third, we wanted to indicate that communal celebrations, sacramental or nonsacramental, need not be confined to the seasons of Advent and Lent. We have applied the principle of penitential celebration to other, less obvious times of the year in order to demonstrate the pastoral possibilities inherent in the new *Rite of Penance* if its spirit is absorbed and understood. We invite you to examine the life of your community and discover additional situations and occasions which would benefit from the celebration of reconciliation.

This book presents two sets of celebrations. The first set in Part I consists of 14 suggested services which we have composed for different occasions in a parish community during the course of a liturgical year. The second set in Part II, consisting of nine sample services, is reprinted from the text of the *Rite of Penance.* The Congregation for Divine Worship prepared these nine celebrations as samples, without wishing to canonize them as official texts. They are merely intended as guides for the creation of similar services, and they should be used as a source for texts and suggestions in your own planning. Part III reprints the "Form of Examination of Conscience" from the *Rite of Penance.*

We have written this book to show you some of the directions which we see indicated in the new *Rite of Penance* for communal services. We are giving you some ideas for your own thinking and planning. It is not a ritual book. Nevertheless, we sincerely hope that it will be of assistance to you in *preparing* to celebrate together with others the reconciliation which God won for us through Jesus Christ.

William J. Freburger
James E. Haas

Part One

———•◦•◦•———

Suggested
Penitential Services

1 Advent

Theme

Advent is a time of the "already" and the "not yet"; Christ has *already* come, but he has *not yet* come again. "We do not preach only one coming of Christ," writes Saint Cyril of Jerusalem, "but a second as well, much more glorious than the first. The first coming was marked by patience; the second will bring the crown of a divine kingdom." The purpose of this celebration is to gather the community in reflection upon the experience of Christ's presence. He has come, and that should have made a difference in our lives. He will come again, and we prepare a response appropriate to that promise.

Preparation

On the two Sundays prior to the celebration, bulletin and pulpit announcements should feature the following invitation: "We invite all parishioners to prepare for the coming of Christ by participating in the communal celebration of the sacrament of Penance on (date) at (time). To ready ourselves for the sacrament and for Christmas, please consider prayerfully during the coming days your own response to the statement: 'One reason why the coming of Christ among us is personally important to me is _____.' "

Immediately before the celebration itself, a sufficient number of forms should be printed with the statement given at the end of the preceding paragraph ("One reason why," etc.). These forms, together with a quantity of pencils, should be placed in the pews before the service starts.

Opening Hymn

"On Jordan's Bank"[1]

Call to Prayer

The celebrant may adapt the thoughts given in the theme statement (above), to introduce the celebration and to invite the participants to pray.

Opening Prayer

God our Father, your Son Jesus Christ has entered our world and transformed its blighted promises into new hope. Send your Spirit upon us gathered here, that we may produce the appropriate fruits of repentance to welcome him who comes, Jesus Christ your Son, who lives and reigns with you and the Holy Spirit, as one God, for ever and ever. Amen.

Liturgy of the Word

1. Romans 13:10-14
2. Matthew 3:1-11

Homily

The celebrant begins by calling attention to the forms in the pews. After pointing out that the coming of Christ cannot leave us neutral, he invites everyone to spend a few moments of silent reflection in responding to the statement on the form. They may write their personal response, but will not be asked to share it with others.

After the time of reflection, the celebrant develops the message of the scripture proclaimed. Now is "the time" (Romans), a critical juncture in our personal histories. The coming of Christ demands an appropriate response (Matthew). The forms reveal what each of us sees as such a response—but is it *appropriate?* Have we settled for mere redecoration or rearrangement of our lives, rather than true conversion of heart?

Examination of Conscience

The homily leads directly into the examination of conscience. The celebrant invites all to kneel and to spend a few moments of silence reviewing their past responses to Christ's presence and their need for renewed dedication in the days and weeks to come.

The Our Father

At the end of the examination of conscience, all stand and the celebrant introduces the praying of the Our Father:

Our God is faithful. He offers us mercy for the past and hope for the future. We now pray for those gifts in the words that Jesus himself taught us:

Our Father, etc.

Individual Confessions and Absolution

If individual confessions are to be celebrated, they take place at this point. The ministers of the sacrament should be alert to the possibilities of helping the individual penitents to articulate an appropriate act of satisfaction ("penance") based on the personal responses elicited by the forms and the examination of conscience.

Thanksgiving and Praise

When the confessions are over, the priests return to the sanctuary, and the celebrant urges all to thank the Lord of mercy by singing in a spirit of hope the hymn, "O Come, O Come, Emmanuel."[2]

Closing Prayer

God our Father, you have enriched us in so many ways. Do not withhold from us any of the gifts of your Spirit while we are waiting for our Lord Jesus Christ to be revealed. Keep us steady and without blame until that day. By calling us, you have joined us to your Son, Jesus Christ our Lord, who lives and reigns with you and the Holy Spirit, as one God, for ever and ever. Amen.

Blessing and Dismissal

(From the *Sacramentary,* "Solemn Blessings," 1. Advent.)

You believe that the Son of God once came to us; you look for him to come again.

15

May his coming bring you the light of his holiness
and free you with his blessing.

R. Amen.

May God make you steadfast in faith,
joyful in hope, and untiring in love
all the days of your life.

R. Amen.

You rejoice that our Redeemer came to live with us as
    man.
When he comes again in glory,
may he reward you with endless life.

R. Amen.

May almighty God bless you,
the Father, and the Son, ✠ and the Holy Spirit.

R. Amen.

2 Holy Family

(at home)

Theme

Eating is a biological necessity; but we human beings have learned to raise that natural necessity to the level of love. When a family gathers around a table, there is evident union and sharing. Meals have a "sacred" quality. Those who eat become conscious that they are receivers. The food they share is a gift to them—from God and from each other. A meal can be a "sacrament" of family life.

Preparation

This celebration is designed to be used by families at home in the context of a meal. We have written the text in such a way that it may be easily transcribed for distribution as a bulletin insert, perhaps on Christmas Day itself as an invitation to families to end the civil year in the spirit of Christmas by making the main meal on Holy Family Sunday a special occasion. The service may be adapted, of course, for other times and seasons.

Explanation

The following paragraph should be printed as a preface to the text of the celebration:

We invite the families of our parish to make the main meal on Holy Family Sunday (December ...., 19....) a special occasion. The year is now ending, and we need to ask forgiveness of God and of each other for our lack of love during the past 12

17

months. What better way to celebrate our need for forgiveness than at a meal during which we can thank God for his mercy and kindness? The whole family should be involved beforehand—in planning the meal, in buying the food, in cooking the dishes, in decorating the table in a festive manner.

Once the meal has been prepared, the family gathers around the table. The head of the household says the following prayer:

God our Father, we thank you for the gift of this past year, and we ask your forgiveness for the times when we have separated ourselves from you and from each other in anger or hatred, in pride or spite. Make this meal a sign of all the good things we want to share in the coming year. We thank you especially for this food, and for the love of all who prepared it. We make this prayer through Christ our Lord. Amen.

The main courses are then served. Once the meal has been eaten, the table is cleared. Before dessert, the head of the household invites all to stand and says:

This food we have shared is God's gift to us. In the bible, whenever Jesus ate a meal, he always blessed his Father for his gifts. We do that now. We bless God our Father for everything he has given us, and we use the words of Saint Paul.

The text of Ephesians 1:3-6 is read. After the reading, the head of the household says:

Let us continue to bless God our Father by asking his forgiveness for our sins of the past year. We look for his grace in the coming year. We join hands and pray the prayer that Jesus taught us:

Our Father, etc.

At the conclusion of the Our Father, the family members exchange an appropriate sign of peace. Then all sit and eat dessert. The meal may end with the singing of "O Come, All Ye Faithful."[3]

3 Holy Family
(in church)

Theme

Many parishes have established the custom of blessing children and/or families on Holy Family Sunday. This service combines that custom with a celebration of reconciliation. Like the preceding family celebration at home, this one in church gathers the families of the parish to seek forgiveness for the sins of the past year and to pray for God's strength to live in his presence through love during the coming year.

Preparation

As with all parish celebrations, this service needs antecedent publicity over a period of time. If the parish has decided to supply families with a bulletin insert containing the home celebration, the sheet could feature in a prominent position an invitation for individual families to join in this parish celebration.

Opening Hymn

"Like Olive Branches"[4]

Call to Prayer

The celebrant may adapt the thoughts given in the theme statement (above), to introduce the celebration and to invite the participants to pray.

Opening Prayer

God our Father, we gather here today as a family of families, the parish of (St.) _____. Although we have dedicated ourselves to love, there is jealousy and ambition in our midst, there is disharmony and evil. Send us your peace and, through your Word, strengthen us to live together in the way that will bear fruit in holiness. This we ask through Christ our Lord. Amen

Liturgy of the Word

1. Ephesians 4:2-7, 15-16
2. John 14:23-27

Homily

The scripture shows how the love we have for each other in our living together is a sign of God's work in our midst. As we look back over the last 12 months, the perspective of time allows us to organize our daily experiences—to see that God was indeed at work in us, to recognize the obstacles we place in the way of his work. We are the people to whom Jesus has made the gospel promise: "My Father and I will come and make our home with you." As we look to the coming year of 19........, we ask God in his mercy to bring us closer together, to forgive our sins, and to bless our families.

Examination of Conscience

The homily should lead directly into the examination of conscience, which is done in litany fashion with a response, "Have pity on me, O God, have pity on me." The celebrant invites all to kneel. He reads each of the questions, as indicated below, leads the participants in the response, and pauses briefly between the questions.

Some of us are fathers. If I am a father, where have I refused to let God be at work in me? For those refusals, let us pray to the Lord.

The other five petitions are similar, with the appropriate family relationships substituted in place of "father": mother, sister, brother, son, daughter.

Our Father

At the end of the examination of conscience, all stand and the celebrant introduces the praying of the Our Father:

Let us ask God to give us his forgiveness for sins of the past year, and his grace for the months of the coming year. As families, we join hands and pray as Jesus taught us:

Our Father, etc.

Individual Confessions and Absolution

If individual confessions are to be celebrated, they take place at this point. The ministers of the sacrament should help each penitent to recognize his or her evil in the context of family life. The act of satisfaction would then flow appropriately from this recognition.

Thanksgiving and Praise

When the confessions are over, the priests return to the sanctuary, and the celebrant urges all to exchange a sign of peace as a way of recognizing God's presence in each other.

Closing Prayer

God our Father, make our love for each other increase more and more. Deepen our knowledge and open our eyes so that we can always recognize what is best. Prepare us for that perfect goodness which Jesus Christ produces in us for your glory and praise, which will resound for ever and ever. Amen.

Blessing and Dismissal

God our Father, we ask you to bless these families. Help us all to be tolerant with each other, following the example of Jesus Christ. Keep us united in mind and voice so that we may always give glory to you, our Father. Give us joy and peace in our faith, and send us the power of your Spirit so that we may never lose hope. We ask this blessing in the name of the Father, ✠ and of the Son, and of the Holy Spirit. Amen.

Closing Hymn

"I Will Celebrate Your Love Forever, Yahweh"[5]

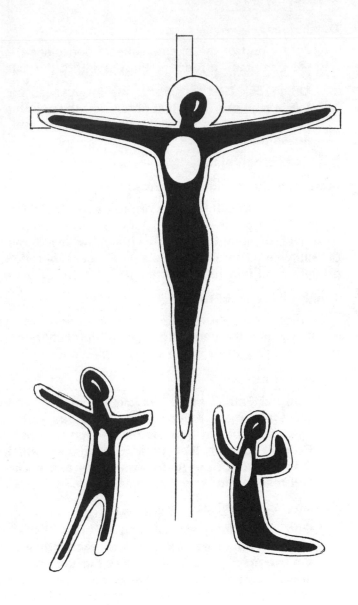

4 Ash Wednesday

Theme

The beginning of Lent is the beginning of conversion. It is merely a first step, which calls for further steps. The taking of ashes is a sign of commitment to that Lenten journey. This celebration integrates that penitential sign with the opportunity to discern where the Lord is calling each of us to go. Why do I need this Lent? What do I lack? Where do I need to grow? To what do I want to commit myself?

Preparation

Ash Wednesday inaugurates the season of Lent with the traditional blessing and distribution of ashes. When this ancient penitential practice occurs outside the Eucharist, the *Sacramentary* directs that it be done within the context of a Liturgy of the Word. It makes no sense to rend our garments unless the Word of God has first rent our hearts. Outside Mass, then, the blessing and distribution of ashes is already a penitential celebration. We have added some touches to the official texts of the *Sacramentary* and the *Lectionary* in order to emphasize the importance of the 40 days that follow Ash Wednesday, and to suggest a number of ways in which the Lenten season may be celebrated more coherently.

First, the parish schedule of Lenten activities should be planned and coordinated well ahead of time. The schedule can then be printed as a brochure for distribution at this

Ash Wednesday celebration. The listing may also include notice of special events, prayer meetings, Lenten devotions, suggested home activities, prospectus of Sunday themes, etc.

Second, the date and time of the penitential celebration for Holy Week should also be decided ahead of time so that the information may be available at the beginning of the season, as a target toward which parishioners may direct their growth in penance. Use the date as a "teaser" in the Sunday bulletin, e.g., "See you on Wednesday, April 6, at 7:30 p.m." You may wish to display a poster or a banner in the church vestibule, from Ash Wednesday on, with a similar legend, e.g., "Wednesday, April 6, 7:30 p.m.—If you're not here, we'll miss you!"

Third, prepare a covenant form for distribution on the Sunday before Ash Wednesday and at this Ash Wednesday celebration. This covenant form is a pledge, a device for deepening the individual's sense of commitment to a penitential way of life during Lent. The text may be simply stated, as follows:

> Our Lord Jesus Christ has saved me from sin and death by his death and resurrection. In order to share more fully in his salvation and to prepare myself for the celebration of Easter, I, _____(name)_____, commit myself to the following during this season of Lent: _____
> _____. May the Lord strengthen me in my resolve to follow him. (Signed)

Call to Prayer

After an appropriate opening hymn, the celebrant may adapt the theme statement (given above) to introduce the celebration and to invite the participants to pray.

Opening Prayer

(From the *Sacramentary.*)

**Lord,
protect us in our struggle against evil.
As we begin the discipline of Lent,
make this season holy by our self-denial.**

Grant this through our Lord Jesus Christ, your Son, who lives and reigns with you and the Holy Spirit, one God, for ever and ever.

Liturgy of the Word

(From the *Lectionary,* no. 220.)

1. Joel 2:12-18
2. 2 Corinthians 5:20-6:2
3. Matthew 6:1-6, 16-18

Homily

Before the celebration begins, the covenant forms (and pencils) should be placed in the pews. At the beginning of the homily, the celebrant calls attention to the forms and presents them as a concrete way of responding to the message of today's readings. He then leads the people into a consideration of the meaning and purpose of Lenten penance. The homily concludes with a brief discussion of the symbol of ashes, and of the seriousness with which they should be taken outwardly as a sign of inner commitment to conversion.

Blessing and Distribution of Ashes

The celebrant blesses the ashes with the prayer given in the *Sacramentary.*

**Dear friends in Christ,
let us ask our Father
to bless these ashes
which we use
as the mark of our repentance.**

**Lord,
bless these ashes ✠
by which we show that we are dust.
Pardon our sins
and keep us faithful to the discipline of Lent,
for you do not want sinners to die
but to live with the risen Christ,
who reigns with you for ever and ever.**

Before inviting people to come forward to accept the ashes, he asks them to spend some moments in silence, reflecting upon the blank spaces on the covenant forms (name, Lenten penance, signature). Are they ready to fill them in? To what will they commit themselves in this Lenten season? He urges them to take their time in this reflection, and to come forward once they have signed and completed their covenant forms.

General Intercessions

After the distribution of ashes, the celebrant washes his hands and leads the people in the praying of a set of appropriate petitions. An appendix of the *Sacramentary* gives a number of sample formulas for the season of Lent. "Lent I" follows:

Introduction

My brothers and sisters,
we should pray at all times,
but especially during this season of Lent;
we should faithfully keep watch with Christ
and pray to our Father.

Intercessions

A. That Christians everywhere
may be responsive to the word of God
during this holy season,
we pray to the Lord:

R. Lord, have mercy.

B. That people everywhere may work for peace
to make these days the acceptable time
of God's help and salvation,
we pray to the Lord:

R. Lord, have mercy.

C. That all who have sinned or grown lukewarm
may turn to God again
during this time of reconciliation,
we pray to the Lord:

R. Lord, have mercy.

D. That we ourselves may learn to repent
   and turn from sin
   with all our hearts,
   we pray to the Lord:

   R. Lord, have mercy.

Concluding Prayer

Lord,
may your people turn again to you
and serve you with all their hearts.
With confidence we have asked your help;
may we now know your mercy and love in our lives.
We ask this through Christ our Lord.

R. Amen.

Final Admonition

After the prayer of the faithful, the celebrant invites the people to sit and addresses them in these words (a paraphrasing of Deuteronomy 30:1-5, 11-14, 19):

The words of mercy which you have heard today will come true for you, if you meditate on them in your heart as the Lord leads you throughout the coming 40 days. If you return to the Lord, if you obey his voice with all your heart and soul in everything you do, then the Lord will have mercy on you.

Even if you have wandered far from God, he can bring you back. He will come to reclaim you. He will change your heart so that you may love him. He will give you life and take delight in you. He will make you in the image of his Son, Jesus Christ.

You have taken the ashes of penance and thereby committed yourself to conversion in this time of Lent. It is not beyond your strength or beyond your reach, for God himself has put his Word in your mouth and in your heart for your observance. Obey his voice and cling to him, for in this your life consists.

Blessing and Dismissal

(From the *Sacramentary*, "Solemn Blessings," 5. Passion of the Lord.)

**The Father of mercies has given us an example of unselfish love
in the sufferings of his only Son.
Through your service of God and neighbor
may you receive his countless blessings.**

R. Amen.

**You believe that by his dying
Christ destroyed death for ever.
May he give you everlasting life.**

R. Amen.

**He humbled himself for our sakes.
May you follow his example
and share in his resurrection.**

R. Amen.

**May almighty God bless you,
the Father, and the Son, ✝ and the Holy Spirit.**

R. Amen.

5 Holy Week

Theme

The journey of Lent has a goal: the participation of each believer in the paschal mystery of Jesus, in spirit and in truth. By dying to sin with Jesus, we come alive with him to God. This celebration is a call to death and resurrection, both for those who have lived Lent in a penitential spirit and for those who have been moved only now to respond to the Lord's love.

Preparation

For the examination of conscience in this celebration, we suggest a visual accompaniment. Its subject is "resurrection in our lives"—those points of our existence where we can experience the power of Jesus' resurrection. The selection and preparation of appropriate slides should be completed a few weeks before the celebration. The location in which the service takes place should be physically suitable for projection. If conditions do not allow the use of audio-visual media, then do not use them!

Throughout the season of Lent, those who signed covenants on Ash Wednesday should be encouraged in their commitment. Others should be invited to join them. The community ought to be reminded periodically of the date and time of this penitential celebration during Holy Week.

Call to Prayer

The church is darkened (if possible) as the service begins. The celebrant enters the bare sanctuary alone, and he pauses to survey the congregation. When everyone is not only quiet but also silent (there is a difference!), he says:

Let me tell you a story.

He then reads, very deliberately and solemnly, Matthew 20:1-15. At the conclusion, he speaks to the people as follows:

My friends, our God is indeed generous. Some of us here tonight have toiled through 40 days of Lent, asking God by prayer and penance to change our hearts. We committed ourselves to this Lenten journey and pledged ourselves by covenant to live this season as a way of seeking the Lord and his mercy.

There are others of us here tonight who have come only now, at the 11th hour.

It does not matter. Whatever our timing, early or late, we are here. And God offers to all of us and to each of us the same thing: forgiveness. No more, but no less. He will lift us all from our sins, he will raise us up.

Let us stand and sing our prayer to this God of mercy.

As the people stand, the other ministers enter and join the celebrant in the sanctuary. If the lights have been dimmed at the beginning, they now come up so that the people may see to sing.

Opening Hymn

"Draw Near, O Lord Our God"[6]

Opening Prayer

God our Father, in your mercy you offer us everything we need for life and faith. You have brought us to know you and you have called us to share your glory. In giving us these gifts you have also given us the guarantee of something great and wonderful still to come. Hear our prayer, and add your holiness to the faith which we already have. We make this prayer through Christ our Lord. Amen.

Liturgy of the Word

Ephesians 2:1-10

Homily

God is generous, but we do not merit his generosity. We need his mercy, but we cannot earn it. He freely forgives us in Christ. What we touch turns to death; the Lord's touch brings us to life. He reaches out to us here tonight to vivify us.

Examination of Conscience

Where do we need resurrection in our lives? The examination of conscience should be prepared as a meditation on that question. A list of the resurrection-experiences that are possible even now could be read, supported by the projection of appropriate slides.

Our Father

At the end of the examination of conscience, all stand, and the celebrant introduces the praying of the Our Father:

We are dead through our sins, but God will bring us to life with his Son, Jesus Christ. Let us pray for his mercy, with the words that Jesus taught us.

Our Father, etc.

Individual Confessions and Absolution

Individual confessions are celebrated at this point. It might be good for the parish liturgy committee to establish beforehand a set of prayers and hymns to be used during this period. These should not be seen as "fillers," but as a way of honoring the counsel of James: "Pray for one another, and this will heal you" (James 5:16).

Thanksgiving and Praise

When the confessions are over, the priests return to the sanctuary, and the celebrant urges all to thank the Lord of mercy for his generosity by singing the hymn, "Now Thank We All Our God."[7]

Closing Prayer

Father, we thank you for removing everything that hinders us, especially the sins that cling so easily. Let us not lose sight of Jesus who leads us in our faith and brings it to perfection. As we have shared his sufferings, may we also share his resurrection. We make this prayer through him who lives and reigns with you and the Holy Spirit, as one God, for ever and ever. Amen.

Blessing and Dismissal

(From the *Sacramentary,* "Solemn Blessings," 12. Ordinary Time III.)

May almighty God bless you in his mercy,
and make you always aware of his saving wisdom.

R. Amen.

May he strengthen your faith with proofs of his love,
so that you will persevere in good works.

R. Amen.

May he direct your steps to himself
and show you how to walk in charity and peace.

R. Amen.

May almighty God bless you,
the Father, and the Son, ✠ and the Holy Spirit.

R. Amen.

6 Pentecost

Theme

In many communities, Pentecost signals a change in the tenor of parish life. The school year is ending, the summer hiatus looms ahead, and the parish council is putting the finishing touches on the pastoral plans and budget for the coming year. Just as the first Pentecost, prepared by prayer, marked a turning point in the life of the Church, so every Pentecost can serve a similar function. This celebration invites the parish to spend time in prayer: considering the past year of community life, searching for the Spirit in the present, and looking to the future with hope.

Preparation

The purpose of this celebration is to create, within the parish, a unity in the Spirit who was given for the forgiveness of sins and the revelation of all truth. Two weeks before Pentecost, the prayerful insight of the total community should be solicited through a form distributed with the Sunday bulletin. The text to be printed is as follows:

> In preparation for the coming of the Spirit, the Apostles gathered to await the first Pentecost. They waited in prayer. On (date) at (time and place), we invite all parishioners to gather in prayer for the coming of the Spirit. At that time, we will ask the Spirit of forgiveness to pour his mercy upon our sins of the past; we will ask the Spirit of hope to pour his courage into our hearts for the future.

> To prepare for this time of prayer, we ask of you three things:

1) Spend your own time in prayer over the next few days considering these questions:

Where has our community hindered the work of the Spirit? _____

What must our parish do in order to welcome the Spirit? _____

2) Fill in the blanks with the results of your praying and return this form to the rectory by mail before next Sunday, or drop it in the collection basket next Sunday.

3) And come to the celebration on (date, as above) at (time and place, as above).

During the week before Pentecost, the parish staff should meet to study the forms prayerfully and to integrate them into the celebration (especially in the homily and the examination of conscience). The staff will take advantage of this occasion to assess the diversity of the parish, with the realization that the unity to be achieved does not destroy differences. A realistic portrait of the parish community will acknowledge both failings and virtues.

Opening Hymn

"Come, Holy Ghost"[8] or "The Spirit Is A'Movin' "[9] or, for greater solemnity, "Veni Creator Spiritus"[10] (with an elaborate entrance procession).

Call to Prayer

Now is Pentecost, the time of the Spirit. The Father will not refuse us any gift that we ask of him, so let us ask him for the Spirit—to heal our past, to sanctify the present, to brighten our future. Let us pray. (Pause for silent prayer.)

Opening Prayer

God our Father, give us your Spirit of power so that we may grow strong and Christ may live in our hearts through faith. Open us to your Word so that we may know completely that love of Christ which is beyond all our human knowledge. This prayer we make through Christ our Lord. Amen.

34

Liturgy of the Word

1. 1 Corinthians 12:4-11
2. John 15:5-9

Homily

The Spirit makes each of us different. He gives each of us a unique gift that distinguishes us from all others, but which makes all of us necessary for each other. And so, he is also the Spirit of unity, who joins us with Jesus and with each other. But differences sometimes weigh more heavily with us than our points of unity. The Spirit, therefore, is the gift of integrity. Where sin divides and alienates, he makes us whole.

The homilist should apply this message to the results of the staff discussion of the forms. What were the differences that divided the community during the past year? What did the forms suggest for the future? What are the priorities to be established, personally and communally, to make those suggestions real?

The homily should make it obvious that the forms which were returned have been taken seriously and prayerfully.

Examination of Conscience

The forms should direct the preparation of the examination of conscience: community failings, individual lack of participation in parish life, etc. If possible, wording of the examination should be taken from the forms.

Our Father

At the end of the examination of conscience, all stand and the celebrant introduces the praying of the Our Father:

The Lord Jesus who is the true vine gave us the words in which to express our need of unity. Let us pray to the Father as Jesus taught us:

Our Father, etc.

Individual Confessions and Absolution

If individual confessions are to be celebrated, they take place at this point. The ministers of the sacrament should be alert to the possibilities of assigning an act of satisfaction

35

appropriate to the theme of the celebration: a gift of time, talent, or enthusiastic prayer for the building of unity in the parish.

Thanksgiving and Praise

When the confessions are over, the priests return to the sanctuary, and the celebrant urges all to thank the Father and Son for making a unity out of our diversity through the gift of the Spirit. The gratitude may be expressed in song: "Bring to the Lord,"[11] "Peace I Leave With You,"[12] etc.

Closing Prayer

Father, our unity comes from you through your Son, Jesus Christ, by the gift of the Holy Spirit. All over the world, you are gathering people to yourself, so that we may always praise your name. In this unity, you manifest what you can do and you show what men and women can be. Our parish must be a sign of what happens when you fall in love with people, and they fall in love with you.

And so, Father, we bring you ourselves. We ask you to make us one in holiness through the power of your Spirit. May we be, always and everywhere, your sons and daughters who pray to you through your Son, Jesus Christ, our Lord, who lives and reigns with you in the unity of the Holy Spirit, as one God, for ever and ever. Amen.

Blessing and Dismissal

(From the *Sacramentary,* "Solemn Blessings," 9. Holy Spirit.)

**(This day) the Father of light
has enlightened the minds of the disciples
by the outpouring of the Holy Spirit.
May he bless you
and give you the gifts of the Spirit for ever.**

R. Amen.

**May that fire which hovered over the disciples
as tongues of flame**

**burn out all evil from your hearts
and make them glow with pure light.**

R. Amen.

**God inspired speech in different tongues
to proclaim one faith.
May he strengthen your faith
and fulfill your hope of seeing him face to face.**

R. Amen.

**May almighty God bless you,
the Father, and the Son, ✠ and the Holy Spirit.**

R. Amen.

After the Celebration

Why not continue the spirit of unity fostered in prayer by gathering the group for fellowship and refreshments in the church hall or school auditorium?

7 End of School Year

Theme

The end of a year is a time for looking back, for summarizing, for evaluating. But it is also a time for looking forward. This celebration is meant to achieve both for a student body. It is a pause in the pilgrimage, as school closes and summer begins.

Preparation

In preparation for the celebration, each class in the school should be asked to do the following:

> 1. To prepare representations (symbol, poster, collage, banner, etc.) of *two* significant events in the experience of the class during the past school year. These representations will be carried in the opening and closing processions, and will be referred to in the homily and the period of praise and thanksgiving.
>
> 2. To prepare a petition for the examination of conscience. The petition should be solicited as a response to the question, "Where can we do better?", and composed in the following format: "That God our Father may help us to
> _____ "

Opening Hymn

"Here We Are."[13] In the procession with the celebrant, representative students carry their classes' representations of the year. The students place these in the sanctuary around the altar and then sit in places reserved for them in the front pews.

Opening Prayer

(After a pause for silent prayer.)

God our Father, you have revealed the mysteries of the kingdom of heaven to us. Bless our memories so that we may know your presence during this past year. Bless our eyes so that we may see you in those around us. Bless our hearts so that we may bring you to those with whom we live. This prayer we make through Christ our Lord. Amen.

Liturgy of the Word

Matthew 11:2-6

Homily

In response to John's question, Jesus gives signs of who he is. We have here today signs of who we have been: the representations of the school year. These signs are reminders for us of what has happened. But they are not the whole story. Much more has occurred during this past year, both good and bad. For the bad, we need to ask forgiveness of God. For the good, we have to praise and thank the Lord.

Examination of Conscience

The celebrant invites all to kneel for the examination of conscience. The petitions, prepared beforehand by each class, may be read by the class representatives sitting in the front pews.

The Our Father

At the end of the examination of conscience all stand and the celebrant introduces the praying of the Our Father:

We present our petitions to God. We are confident that he will hear us, for he is the Lord of mercy. That is why we call him:

Our Father, etc.

Individual Confessions and/or Sign of Peace

At this point, individual confessions may be celebrated, if desired. However, the size of the student body and the percentage of those who have not yet received first Penance may indicate the advantage of offering the sacrament at another time—immediately after this celebration or later in the school day. In place of confessions, then, the students are invited to exchange a sign of peace and reconciliation.

Praise and Thanksgiving

The class representatives are invited forward. Each one takes a class symbol and holds it up as the assembly sings an appropriate song of thanksgiving for the blessings of the past year.

Closing Prayer

God our Father, we thank you for your many gifts of this past year. Your faithful presence has helped us to grow in wisdom and love. Be with us in the coming months of summer so that we may continue to be your children who pray to you through our Lord, Jesus Christ, your Son, who lives and reigns with you and the Holy Spirit, as one God, for ever and ever. Amen.

Blessing and Dismissal

(From the *Sacramentary,* "Solemn Blessings," 10, Ordinary Time I. Blessing of Aaron — Num 6:24-26)

May the Lord bless you and keep you.

R. Amen.

**May his face shine upon you,
and be gracious to you.**

R. Amen.

**May he look upon you with kindness,
and give you his peace.**

R. Amen.

**May almighty God bless you,
the Father, and the Son, ✠ and the Holy Spirit.**

R. Amen.

Closing Hymn

"Be a New Man,"[14] by Joe Wise. In the closing procession, the class representatives leave with the celebrant as they carry the symbols.

8 Midsummer

Theme

In most regions of this country, the summer months are a lethargic time. The heat seems to slow everybody, including parish communities. "You can't get people out in the summer," is the usual reason for a light schedule of activities. This celebration takes advantage of the summer spirit. It invites people out: to gather as families and to re-create themselves both spiritually and physically.

Preparation

This celebration is intended for the latter part of the summer, for two hours on a Friday or Saturday afternoon or evening. It aims at families but it is not restricted to them. The two hours are divided into three parts:

1. A "retreat" experience (25 minutes)

Children and adults, separated into respective groups, spend some time in considering the effect of summer on themselves and the people with whom they share life.

2. The penitential celebration (20 minutes)

After a brief recess, the two groups reunite for the celebration which emphasizes the refreshing qualities of water on the physical and spiritual levels.

3. A picnic meal (60 minutes)

At the end of the celebration, everyone gathers
—outdoors, if possible—for an informal meal.
The parish can supply the basics, a "covered
dish" sharing may take care of the rest.

The talents of the liturgical committee as well as of the
teachers in the school and C.C.D. should be utilized in
planning the "retreat" experience for the children and the
adults. Preparation for this two-hour celebration must take
into account the various locations in which the parts will
occur, so that movement between them may take place
easily, with a minimum of confusion or delay. As always,
antecedent publicity must begin far in advance of the scheduled date; it should be frequent, and sufficiently varied and
intriguing to gain attention. Finally, paper and drawing materials will be needed in the course of the "retreat" experience.

The "Retreat" Experience

By using the word "retreat," we do not mean to imply
somberness. It is a "retreat" in the sense that it allows those
who participate to step back from everyday life in order to
see it better in the light of God's Word. The adults and the
children are to be separated into two groups. The outline
given below is intended for both groups: therefore, it will
have to be adapted to the two levels by the planning committee. Although we suggest that this total celebration be
family-oriented, it may be necessary to take into account the
presence of childless families or single adults. This "retreat"
experience has four parts:

1. A brief presentation, "What Is Summer?" (10 minutes)

Nat King Cole's "Roll Out Those Lazy, Hazy
Days of Summer" has become a kind of national
radio anthem to herald the arrival of summer-
time. "Hazy" and "lazy" are the two character-
istics of these months: the weather warms up
and we slow down. In this way, summer gives us
the chance to re-charge, to re-create, to play, to
enjoy ourselves.

2. Activity, "What kind of summer has it been for you?" (5 minutes)

The opening presentation leads to the question, "What's your summer been like?" The groups should be invited to answer it: the children, by making a drawing representative of their vacation experience; the adults, either by a drawing or by a list of words that describes their summer. The results of this activity should be saved by the participants and brought to the celebration; they will be exchanged within families during the sign of peace.

3. Continuation of presentation, "The people with whom you share the summer" (5 minutes)

The next stage of the experience leads the groups to think about the role of other people in making summer what it is. For the children, the discussion may be somewhat free-form; the adults may have to be more directed. The question to be presented is, "The people with whom you live—what difference have they made for you this summer?"

4. Reflection, "What difference would you like them to make?" (5 minutes)

The "retreat" experience concludes with this opportunity to reflect on the possibilities of growth which summer can provide. These months do give us more time to spend with each other. How can we all work to make this unity better than it has been?

After the "retreat" experience, there should be a five-minute break to allow families to regroup. If possible, all may gather in one place to move together into the space for the celebration. This will provide an evident sign of unity as the second part begins.

Call to Prayer

We have spent some time in reflecting on how summer can refresh us and re-create us. Now, we will see how

44

the Lord refreshes us. He is present to us in all seasons with his power, for he loves us. Let us ask him to be present here among us. (Pause for silent prayer.)

Opening Prayer

The celebrant prays spontaneously, in his own words, in order to catch the mood of the gathering.

Liturgy of the Word

1. Ezekiel 36:25-27
2. John 4:5-15

Homily

In the hot months of summer, cool water is the most refreshing thing we seek: we drink it, we swim in it. Water is the most refreshing thing God offers us all year: the water of Baptism, the water of his mercy and love. As Jesus says in the gospel, "God's water is eternally refreshing."

Examination of Conscience

The celebrant invites all to stand and reminds them of the point made in the "retreat" experience, that the people with whom we share life are part of the refreshment of the summer. How can God's refreshment increase our unity and love over the remaining weeks of summer?

Our Father

After the examination of conscience, the celebrant introduces the praying of the Our Father:

Let us join hands and ask God our Father to refresh us always with his gifts. We use the words that Jesus taught us:

Our Father, etc.

Blessing and Sprinkling of Water

After the Our Father, the celebrant blesses water and sprinkles the assembly according to the formula given in the *Sacramentary* at the penitential rite of Mass.

Sign of Peace

When the celebrant completes the sprinkling, he invites everyone to exchange a sign of peace and to share the results of the activity (drawing or list) during the "retreat" experience.

Blessing and Dismissal

(From the *Sacramentary,* "Prayers Over the People," 2.)

**Lord,
grant your people your protection and grace.
Give them health of mind and body,
perfect love for one another,
and make them always faithful to you.**

Grant this through Christ our Lord.

After the Celebration

At the conclusion, all proceed to the area designated for the picnic meal.

9 Opening of School Year

Theme

Beginnings already contain their conclusions. This celebration, together with its preparation, offers an opportunity for students to begin the school year by setting goals for growth and to dedicate themselves to the achievement of those goals.

Preparation

During the first few days of school, teachers take the time to sketch out for the students a rough map of the year's academic journey. In preparation for this celebration, that setting of academic goals should be integrated with the elaboration of spiritual goals by the students. The parish priests can assist the teachers in facilitating this preparation.

The students should be invited to look back over the past year: what kind of school year did they have? what was their academic strong point? their weak point? They should also consider their summer experience: what kind of persons have they been—alone, with family, with friends, etc.? Over all this time, what has been their relationship to God? Have they cultivated it, or neglected it?

The answers to these questions contain the raw materials of goals toward which the individual students can work. This goal-setting should also be done on the class level: what kind of spiritual program might the class determine for itself? The students could decide, for instance, on a more

47

conscious effort to work in the community or to contribute time to a parish project.

Each class may also compose a petition for the examination of conscience. The content should look both to the past and to the future, according to this pattern: "For the times when we did/didn't _____
and for the grace to/not to (repeat appropriate wording from first insert), we pray to the Lord."

Opening Hymn

"God Has Visited His People"[15]

Call to Prayer

As we come together, we remind ourselves that God has promised us his presence. He comes to us because he loves us. Here today, we will dedicate ourselves. We will seek God's strength so that we can bring him to others. We will ask him to show us the ways to accomplish that in the coming months. Let us pray, then, for his vision and his power. (Pause for silent prayer.)

Opening Prayer

God our Father, we are beginning a journey and we ask you to guide our steps along the way. Please be with us, so that we may continue to grow in your love. This prayer we make through Christ our Lord. Amen.

Liturgy of the Word

Matthew 7:21-27

Homily

Jesus speaks about the right way of beginning: meaning what we say, doing the Father's will, building on substantial foundations. We are beginning a school year, and Jesus' advice comes to us at the proper moment. As we look to the future, we remind ourselves how many times in the past we said, "Lord, Lord," and didn't mean it, how many times we neglected to do the will of God, how many times we built on sand and watched the tide wash our project away. We need to ask the Lord for his forgiveness for the past and his strength for the future.

Examination of Conscience

The homily leads directly into the examination of conscience. The celebrant invites all to kneel. Class representatives may come forward to present the petitions composed by each class.

The Our Father

At the end of the examination of conscience, all stand and the celebrant introduces the praying of the Our Father:

God is faithful and has promised us that, when we ask for the strength to do his will, he will give us power. Let us pray for that strength, using the words that Jesus taught us:

Our Father, etc.

Individual Confessions and/or Sign of Peace

At this point, individual confessions may be celebrated, if desired. However, the size of the student body and the percentage of those not yet initiated into Penance may indicate the advantage of offering the sacrament at another time —immediately after this celebration or later in the school day. In place of confessions, then, the students are invited to exchange a suitable sign of peace and reconciliation.

Praise and Thanksgiving

After the confessions and/or the sign of peace, the students are invited to sing an appropriate hymn of praise to God who supports us on our journey into the future.

Closing Prayer

Father, this is what we pray: help us to grow strong in Christ, by building on the rock of his love. Then who we are and what we do will reveal the breadth and the length, the height and the depth of your power. This prayer we make through Christ our Lord. Amen.

Blessing and Dismissal

(From the *Sacramentary,* "Solemn Blessings," 3, Beginning of the New Year.)

Every good gift comes from the Father of light.

May he grant you his grace and every blessing,
and keep you safe throughout the coming year.

R. Amen.

May he grant you unwavering faith,
constant hope, and love that endures to the end.

R. Amen.

May he order your days and work in his peace,
hear your every prayer,
and lead you to everlasting life and joy.

R. Amen.

May almighty God bless you,
the Father, and the Son, ✠ and the Holy Spirit.

R. Amen.

Closing Hymn

"I'm Ready to Follow"[16]

The following three celebrations are intended for use during a parish program of preparation for first Penance:

1. Preparation for Penance — Adults
2. Preparation for Penance — Children
3. First Penance — Adults and Children

The first two celebrations are nonsacramental; their purpose is to ready each group, adults and children, on their own levels for the third celebration in which the children, together with their parents, will receive the sacrament of reconciliation for the first time. The first two celebrations should be scheduled closely together so as to facilitate their impact on individual families.

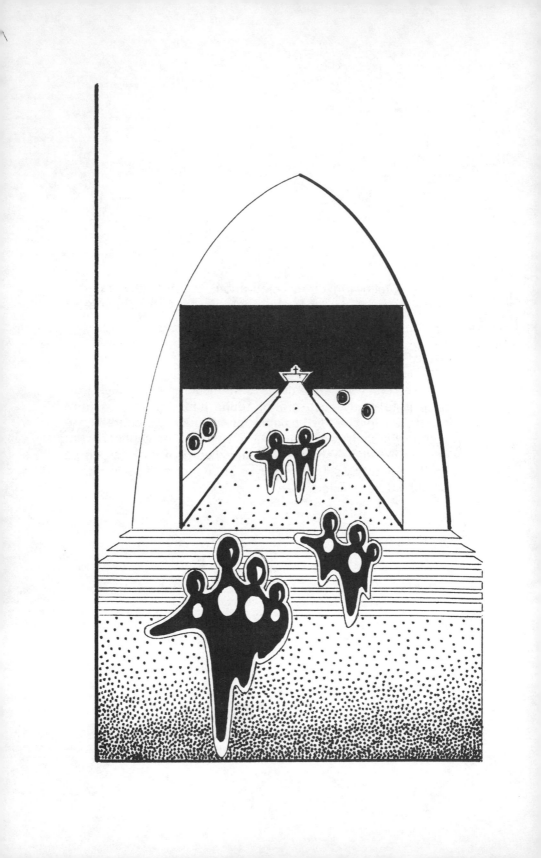

10 Preparation for Penance

(adults)

Theme

It is a truism to say that the family is the school of love. To describe that statement as a truism is not to say that it is false, just that it is obvious. Within the family, the leadership of the adults—whether father or mother or parent without partner—makes growth in love possible. Adults are the environment, the example, the foundation for the love learned by children. This celebration invites those parents to re-affirm their love in the light of faith.

Preparation

This celebration should conclude one of the evening sessions for the parents during the course of the preparation program. Since it comes at the end of an evening's activities, the service should be brief and simple. A few of the 30-second Franciscan Telespots[17] on the subject of family love could serve admirably as mood-setters and as a transition between the session and the celebration.

Call to Worship

(As a lead-in from the Telespots):

Love in the family—that is what we are all about: show-ing love and showing *how* to love. We are preparing our children for love. But let's take the time to prepare ourselves. For a few brief moments now, as we con-clude this evening's activities, we turn to the Lord. Our hearts will be empty . . . unless he fills them. Our hands

will be powerless . . . unless he strengthens them. Our homes will be cold . . . unless he warms them. Let us pray, then, for all the good things the Lord has promised us. Please stand.

Opening Hymn

"Where Charity and Love Prevail"[18]

Opening Prayer

Spontaneously composed by celebrant, to catch the mood of the group.

Liturgy of the Word

1. Romans 12:1-5, 9-18
2. Matthew 7:9-11

Homily

We want the best for our children. Initially, we set no limits—aside from those inherent in our finiteness—to the giving or the saving or the sacrificing that is necessary to obtain good things for our children. Even our participation in this program is another sign of that parental generosity. But there is an expensive gift, within our reach, which we often overlook. It is expensive in terms of the cost to each of us personally. It is expensive but easily obtainable. The gift is— yourself! Of all the good things we have to give to each other, this is the gift that means the most.

Examination of Conscience

With a lead-in from the homily, this examination of conscience takes the form of a brief period of reflection on the following questions:

What good things have we withheld from our children? from each other?

Have we withheld time? enthusiasm? talents? words of praise?

Have we used a double standard, i.e., preached much but practiced little?

Have we stolen the sense of wonder from our children and given them only the taste for cynicism in return?

Have we hidden God from our children and from each other?

Have we withheld from each other our greatest gift: ourselves?

The Our Father

After the examination of conscience, all stand and the celebrant introduces the praying of the Our Father:

The Father loves us and he will give us all the good things we ask of him. We look to him for mercy and we pray with the words that Jesus taught us:

Our Father, etc.

Sign of Peace

At the end of the Our Father, the celebrant invites the group to exchange a sign of peace:

The Lord has forgiven us; now we must forgive each other. Let us embrace in peace and take the same gift to our children this very night.

Closing Prayer

God our Father, clothe us richly in compassion, kindness and humility. Help us to forgive each other as soon as a quarrel starts. May the peace of Christ fill our hearts and our homes. For all your gifts, we give you thanks through our Lord Jesus Christ, your Son, who lives and reigns with you and the Holy Spirit, as one God, for ever and ever. Amen.

Blessing and Dismissal

(The tripartite blessing of parents adapted from the *Rite of Baptism for Children.*)

God the Father, through his Son, the Virgin Mary's child, has brought joy to all Christian mothers, as they see the hope of eternal life shine on their children. They now thank God for the gift of their children. May they be one with them in thanking him for ever in heaven, in Christ Jesus our Lord.

All: Amen.

God is the giver of all life, human and divine. May he bless the fathers of children. With their wives they are the first teachers of their children in the ways of faith. May they be also the best of teachers, bearing witness to the faith by what they say and do, in Christ Jesus our Lord.

All: Amen.

By God's gift, through water and the Holy Spirit, we are reborn to everlasting life. In his goodness, may he continue to pour out his blessings upon all present, who are his sons and daughters. May he make them always, wherever they may be, faithful members of his holy people. May he send his peace upon all who are gathered here, in Christ Jesus our Lord.

All: Amen.

May almighty God, the Father, and the Son, ✠ and the Holy Spirit, bless you.

All: Amen.

11 Preparation for Penance
(children)

Theme

The family is a unity to the extent that each member contributes to the oneness and love. This celebration offers children preparing for first Penance the opportunity to consider their role in the circle of love.

Preparation

This celebration should be scheduled during the preparation for first Penance, in conjunction with the preceding celebration for parents. Teachers and celebrants are to note especially the free-form Liturgy of the Word outlined below. A pad of newsprint and a Magic Marker will be needed for the celebration.

Opening Hymn

Choose an appropriate penitential hymn, known to the children.

Call to Prayer

God loves us and wants us to love him and each other. Let's be silent now and pray to God, each of us in our hearts, to tell him how we want to love him.

Opening Prayer

God our Father, your Son Jesus Christ is the sign of your love for us, for our families, and for all people in the world. Hear our prayers and help us to love you and each other better. We ask this through Christ our Lord. Amen.

Liturgy of the Word

After the opening prayer the celebrant invites the children to be seated and asks them to list groups to which they belong (Scouts, sports teams, etc.). As the names are suggested, he writes them on the newsprint. Each of these groups has a good goal toward which it strives and standards that are to be met by those who participate. The celebrant may solicit from the children some of these goals and standards, to be listed on the newsprint next to the group to which they refer.

Even though the groups have these goals and standards, individuals who belong to the groups do not always live up to them. At this point, the celebrant reads Mark 9:33-35 and asks the children to comment on the attitude of the disciples (who are obviously not concerned with Jesus' standards).

It is difficult to admit that we have not lived up to the goals of our group. Our family is a group to which we belong; the Church is a group to which we belong. But in our families and in our Church, what happens when we fail? Are we thrown out? No, we are still loved and welcomed, because our families and our God want the best for us. When we fail, their love still accepts us and helps us to do better.

Examination of Conscience

On a fresh piece of newsprint, the celebrant lists suggestions from the children in response to the question: "What are the things that make a person 'a member of the team' in the family?" The list should include not just tasks but also attitudes. Invite the children to select from the list, during a moment of reflection, the one thing that each of them needs to do better.

The Our Father

We now need God's help to carry out what we have chosen from the list. Let's pray for that help as Jesus taught us:

Our Father, etc.

Praise and Thanksgiving

Choose an appropriate song, joyful in tone.

Closing Prayer

God our Father, be with us everywhere and strengthen our hearts to love as Jesus showed us. He is the Lord who lives and reigns with you and the Holy Spirit, as one God, for ever and ever. Amen.

Blessing and Dismissal

(From the *Sacramentary,* "Solemn Blessings," 10, Ordinary Time I. Blessing of Aaron — Num 6:24-26)

May the Lord bless you and keep you.

R. Amen.

**May his face shine upon you,
and be gracious to you.**

R. Amen.

**May he look upon you with kindness,
and give you his peace.**

R. Amen.

**May almighty God bless you,
the Father, and the Son, ✠ and the Holy Spirit.**

R. Amen.

Closing Song

Choose a suitable hymn, known to the children.

12 First Penance

(adults and children)

Theme

What does it mean to *celebrate* the sacrament of Penance? The joy of celebrating flows, of course, not from our sins but from God's forgiveness. God does not overlook our evil; he does not forget us. He forgives us. Parents and children gather for this *celebration* to share that experience of being forgiven, not forgotten.

Preparation

If the parents and children have participated in the two preparatory celebrations, that should be taken into account in the planning of this service. In particular, the themes and the previous examinations of conscience might well be integrated into this conclusion of the preparation for first Penance.

Pieces of yarn, four to five inches long, should be prepared for distribution to each person, adult or child, who takes part. As families enter the church, each member receives a length of yarn.

Opening Hymn

"I Must Remember"[19]

60

Call to Prayer

We gather here to celebrate God's forgiveness in the Church. He is a loving God. He does not forget us, he forgives us. We ask him to give us his love, so that we may know the joy of salvation. Let us pray.

(Pause for silent prayer.)

Opening Prayer

God our Father, we remember your promises to your Church. You sent your Son Jesus Christ to be always the sign and source of your mercy. Hear our prayers and share with us your forgiveness, which comes to us through your Son Jesus Christ, our Lord, who lives and reigns with you and the Holy Spirit, as one God, for ever and ever. Amen.

Liturgy of the Word

1. Isaiah 49:12-15
2. Luke 12:22-32

Homily

The obvious message of the readings is that God does not forget us: he loves us with an everlasting love. In our human experience, that love manifests itself as forgiveness. "Manifests"—because that is the purpose of this celebration and of everything that has led up to it. These are signs of God's continuing care and concern, signs of his forgiveness. We come together to make these signs because of the pledge we make each time we pray the Our Father: that we must forgive each other, if God is to forgive us. We now call to mind our sins because it is here that God will be active.

Examination of Conscience

At the end of the homily, the celebrant invites all to kneel for the examination of conscience. The petitions may be prepared ahead of time, according to the format: "Lord, we have forgotten the times that we _____; don't count the times, just forgive us, we pray to you," followed by an appropriate response. Since the assembly is composed of adults and children, the petitions should be mixed to represent the age levels present.

The Our Father

After the examination of conscience, all stand and the celebrant introduces the praying of the Our Father:

Jesus taught us a special prayer for forgiveness. Since we are seeking the Lord's forgiveness in a special way, let's pray the words that Jesus gave us:

Our Father, etc.

Individual Confessions and Absolution

Individual confessions are celebrated at this point. It might be well to brief the individual confessors, before the celebration, on the type of preparation which the children have had for the ritual. With this knowledge, the confessors will be able to use the vocabulary known to the children, in order to give explanations or clear up confusions.

Praise and Thanksgiving

Once the confessions are over and the ministers have returned to the sanctuary, the celebrant alludes to the custom of tying a piece of string on one's finger as a mnemonic device. He then invites the congregation to turn toward one another and tie the yarn on one another's fingers, while saying: "Remember—you're forgiven, not forgotten."

All then join in singing "I Will Not Forget You."[20]

Closing Prayer

God our Father, we rejoice in your mercy and we thank you for your love. Keep us always faithful within the family of your people, the Church. Help us to share your forgiveness with others, so that one day all people may gather in your kingdom, where you live with your Son, Jesus Christ, and the Holy Spirit, as one God, for ever and ever. Amen.

Blessing and Dismissal

(From the *Rite of Penance,* no. 213.)

**May the Father bless us,
for we are his children, born to eternal life.**

R. Amen.

**May the Son show us his saving power,
for he died and rose for us.**

R. Amen.

**May the Spirit give us his gift of holiness
and lead us by the right path,
for he dwells in our hearts.**

R. Amen.

Closing Song

Choose an appropriate song, known to everyone.

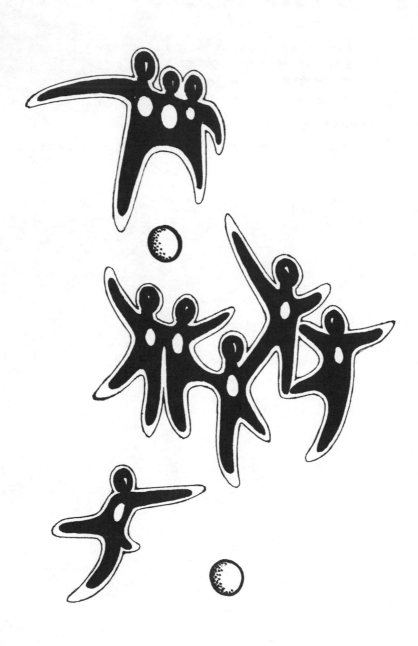

13 Special Education

Theme

"Everyone has his own good gift"—but we do not always share with others the gifts the Lord gives us. What good gifts does a special person have? The gifts may be simple things: singing, dancing, smiling, etc. This celebration invites the children to consider their gifts and not to withhold them selfishly from others.

Preparation

This is a very simple celebration, but it demands a celebrant who appreciates special people and who knows how to lead them in worship. The decision to offer individual confessions should be discussed with the teacher(s) who will be aware of each child's level of progress in catechesis.

Opening Hymn

"Care Is All It Takes"[21]

Call to Prayer

God has given us gifts, and he has given us the strength to gain other gifts through work, study or accomplishment. Let us begin by asking God to help us to appreciate the gifts he has given to each of us.

Opening Prayer

God our Father, we thank you for all your gifts. Help us to share these gifts with others so that they too can rejoice in your kindness to us. We ask this through Christ our Lord. Amen.

Liturgy of the Word

    1. 1 Peter 4:10-11

    2. Mark 12:28-30

Homily

God always gives his gifts in love, to be used in love. The celebrant leads the children to appreciate this by helping them to determine the various gifts represented in the group. Accomplishment should not be emphasized to the detriment of the internal giving from the heart.

Examination of Conscience

The homily leads directly into the examination of conscience. The celebrant repeats the list of gifts solicited during the homily, incorporating them into the following format:

For the times when we didn't   _____ **and could have helped somebody else, we ask you to forgive us, Lord.**

The Our Father

The celebrant introduces the praying of the Our Father:

Jesus gave us a prayer in which we ask God for his gifts, including the gift of forgiveness. Let's pray as he taught us:

Our Father, etc.

Individual Confessions

If it has been decided to offer individual confessions and absolution, they are celebrated at this time.

Praise and Thanksgiving

The celebrant invites the children to share a gift with their neighbors—a smile, a handshake, a pat on the back, words of kindness, etc.

Closing Prayer

God our Father, give us your blessing so that we may recognize all your good gifts; give us your strength so that we can love others with these gifts. We ask this through Christ our Lord. Amen.

Blessing and Dismissal

(From the *Rite of Penance,* no. 58.)

**May the Lord guide your hearts in the way of his love
and fill you with Christ-like patience.**

R. Amen.

**May he give you strength
to walk in newness of life
and to please him in all things.**

R. Amen.

**May almighty God bless you,
the Father, and the Son, ✠ and the Holy Spirit.**

R. Amen.

Closing Song

Choose an appropriate song, familiar to the children.

14   Traditional Holy Hour

Theme

Jesus in the Eucharist is the eternal high priest who has offered himself for the forgiveness of sins. He is the glorified mediator who always makes intercession for us at the right hand of the Father. This celebration invites the participants to adore the Lord in the sacrament and to seek the reconciliation with the Father and others which he offers.

Preparation

In June 1976, without much fanfare, the rite for *Holy Communion and Worship of the Eucharist Outside Mass* went into effect. This document gathers into one place all the disparate liturgical reforms of the past decade affecting the Eucharist, and now regulates the worship and devotion of the sacrament outside the context of the celebration of Mass. Exposition merely for the giving of benediction is forbidden; time must be allowed for reflection on the Word of God, for silent prayer and for adoration. This celebration takes the form of a "holy hour." It incorporates the official revision of benediction with the opportunity to celebrate sacramental reconciliation.

Opening Hymn

"Lord, Who at Thy First Eucharist."[22] The celebrant enters. He brings the sacrament to the altar facing the people and places it in the monstrance which sits on the table of the altar. He then incenses the sacrament while an appropriate eucharistic hymn is sung. After a period of adoration in silence, all are seated.

Liturgy of the Word

1. Exodus 16:2-4, 12-15
2. John 6:24-35

Homily

The problem with "junk food" is that it fills us up without nourishing us. It gives us the semblance of eating without the benefits. Sin is like that: it is the "junk food" of the spirit. Evil is attractive and appetizing, but its effect is deadening. The nourishment that God offers us is *real* food, not an imitation. His gift is so great that it takes us beyond death. What he offers us is his Son Jesus Christ.

Examination of Conscience

At the conclusion of the homily, the celebrant invites the assembly to spend some time in silence reflecting on the ways in which they have attempted to satisfy their "hunger" or slake their "thirst" with sin, instead of with the bread of life.

Intercessions

After the time of reflection, the celebrant leads the participants in an appropriate set of general intercessions, for instance, those given in the *Liturgy of the Hours* for the solemnity of Corpus Christi.

Adoration and Individual Confessions

The Liturgy of the Word is followed by a period of silent adoration during which individual confessions may be celebrated by those who wish to enter more fully into the sacramental reconciliation brought about by the death and resurrection of Jesus.

Benediction

The "holy hour" concludes with benediction. The celebrant goes to the altar, genuflects, and kneels. As he incenses the sacrament, an appropriate eucharistic hymn is sung, for instance, "Pange lingua,"[23] or one of its translations.[24]

After the hymn, the celebrant stands and says one of the prayers (numbers 98, 224-229) from the rite for *Holy Communion and Worship of the Eucharist Outside Mass.*

Lord Jesus Christ,
you gave us the eucharist
as the memorial of your suffering and death.
May our worship of this sacrament of your body and blood
help us to experience the salvation you won for us
and the peace of the kingdom
where you live with the Father and the Holy Spirit,
one God, for ever and ever.

R. Amen.

He then blesses the people with the sacrament.

Closing Hymn

As the celebrant replaces the sacrament in the tabernacle, the people sing a hymn or an acclamation, for instance, *Father, We Thank Thee.*[25]

Part Two

———•–•–•———

Sample
Penitential Services

Appendix II, Rite of Penance

PREPARING PENITENTIAL CELEBRATIONS

1. Penitential celebrations, mentioned in the *Rite of Penance* (nos. 36-37), are beneficial in fostering the spirit and virtue of penance among individuals and communities; they also help in preparing for a more fruitful celebration of the sacrament of penance. However, the faithful must be reminded of the difference between these celebrations and sacramental confession and absolution.[1]

2. The particular conditions of life, the manner of speaking, and the educational level of the congregation or special group should be taken into consideration. Thus liturgical commissions[2] and individual Christian communities preparing these celebrations should choose the texts and format most suited to the circumstances of each particular group.

3. To this end, several examples of penitential celebrations are given below. These are models and should be adapted to the specific conditions and needs of each community.

4. When the sacrament of penance is celebrated in these services, it follows the readings and homily, and the rite of reconciling several penitents with individual confession and absolution is used (nos. 54-59, *Rite of Penance);* when permitted by law, the rite of general confession and absolution is used (nos. 60-63, *Rite of Penance).*

---

[1]See Congregation for the Doctrine of the Faith, *Normae pastorales circa absolutionem sacramentalem generali modo impertiendam,* June 16, 1972, no. X: *AAS* 64 (1972) 513.
[2]See Congregation of Rites, Instruction *Inter Oecumenici,* September 26, 1964, no. 39: *AAS* (1964) 110.

I Penitential Celebrations During Lent

5.   Lent is the principal time of penance both for individual Christians and for the whole Church. It is therefore desirable to prepare the Christian community for a fuller sharing in the paschal mystery by penitential celebrations during Lent.[1]

6.   Texts from the lectionary and sacramentary may be used in these penitential celebrations; the penitential nature of the liturgy of the word in the Masses for Lent should be considered.

7.   Two outlines of penitential celebrations suitable for Lent are given here. The first emphasizes penance as strengthening or restoring baptismal grace; the second shows penance as a preparation for a fuller sharing in the Easter mystery of Christ and his Church.

First Example: PENANCE LEADS TO A STRENGTHENING OF BAPTISMAL GRACE

8.   a)   After an appropriate song and the greeting by the minister, the meaning of this celebration is explained to the people. It prepares the Christian community to recall their baptismal grace at the Easter Vigil and to reach newness of life in Christ through freedom from sins.

---

[1]See Second Vatican Council, constitution *Sacrosanctum Concilium*, no. 109; Paul VI, Apostolic Constitution *Paenitemini*, February 17, 1966, no. IX: *AAS* 58 (1966) 185.

PRAYER

9. b)

> My brothers and sisters, we have neglected the gifts of our baptism and fallen into sin. Let us ask God to renew his grace within us as we turn to him in repentance.
>
> Let us kneel *(or:* Bow your heads before God).

All pray in silence for a brief period.

> Let us stand *(or:* Raise your heads).
>
> Lord Jesus,
> you redeemed us by your passion
> and raised us to new life in baptism.
> Protect us with your unchanging love
> and share with us the joy of your resurrection,
> for you live and reign for ever and ever.
>
> R. Amen.

READINGS

10. c)

First Reading
1 Corinthians 10:1-13   All this that happened to the people of Moses in the desert was written for our benefit.

Responsorial Psalm
Psalm 106:6-10, 13-14, 19-22
>   R *(4):* Lord, remember us,
>   for the love you bear your people.

Gospel
Luke 15:4-7   Share my joy: I have found my lost sheep.

Or:

Luke 15:11-32   Your brother here was dead, and has come to life.

HOMILY

11. d)

The celebrant may speak about:

— the need to fulfill the grace of baptism by living faithfully the Gospel of Christ (see *1 Corinthians 10:1-13);*
— the seriousness of sin committed after baptism (see *Hebrews 6:4-8);*
— the unlimited mercy of our God and Father who continually welcomes those who turn back to him after having sinned (see *Luke 15);*
— Easter as the feast when the Church rejoices over the Christian initiation of catechumens and the reconciliation of penitents.

EXAMINATION OF CONSCIENCE

12. e)

After the homily, the examination of conscience takes place; a sample text is given in Appendix III, page 121. A period of silence should always be included so that each person may personally examine his conscience. In a special way the people should examine their conscience on the baptismal promises which will be renewed at the Easter Vigil.

ACT OF REPENTANCE

13. f)

The deacon (or another minister, if there is no deacon) speaks to the assembly:

My brothers and sisters, the hour of God's favor draws near, the day of his mercy and of our salvation, when death was destroyed and eternal life began. This is the season for planting new vines in God's vineyard, the time for pruning the vines to ensure a richer harvest.

We all acknowledge that we are sinners. We are moved to penance, encouraged by the example and prayers of our brothers and sisters. We admit our guilt and say:

"Lord, I acknowledge my sins; my offenses are always before me. Turn away your face, Lord, from my sins, and blot out all my wrong-doing. Give me back the joy of your salvation and give me a new and steadfast spirit."

We are sorry for having offended God by our sins. May he be merciful and hear us as we ask to be restored to his friendship and numbered among the living who share the joy of Christ's risen life.

Then the priest sprinkles the congregation with holy water, while all sing (say):

Cleanse us, Lord, from all of our sins;
Wash us, and we shall be whiter than snow.

Then the priest says:

Lord our God,
you created us in love
and redeemed us in mercy.
While we were exiled from heaven
by the jealousy of the evil one,
you gave us your only Son,
who shed his blood to save us.
Send now your Holy Spirit
to breathe new life into your children,
for you do not want us to die
but to live for you alone.
You do not abandon those who abandon you;
correct us as a Father
and restore us to your family.

Lord,
your sons and daughters stand before you
in humility and trust.
Look with compassion on us
as we confess our sins.
Heal our wounds;
stretch out a hand of pity

to save us and raise us up.
Keep us free from harm
as members of Christ's body,
as sheep of your flock,
as children of your family.
Do not allow the enemy
to triumph over us
or death to claim us for ever,
for you raised us to new life in baptism.

Hear, Lord, the prayers we offer from contrite hearts.
Have pity on us as we acknowledge our sins.
Lead us back to the way of holiness.
Protect us now and always
from the wounds of sin.
May we ever keep safe in all its fullness
the gift your love once gave us
and your mercy now restores.

We ask this through our Lord Jesus Christ, your Son,
who lives and reigns with you and the Holy Spirit,
one God for ever and ever.

R. Amen.

The celebration ends with an appropriate song and the dismissal of the people.

Second Example: PENANCE PREPARES FOR A FULLER SHARING IN THE PASCHAL MYSTERY OF CHRIST FOR THE SALVATION OF THE WORLD

14.   a)   After an appropriate song and the greeting by the minister, the faithful are briefly reminded that they are linked with each other in sin and in repentance so that each should take his calling to conversion as an occasion of grace for the whole community.

PRAYER

15.   b)

> **My brothers and sisters, let us pray that by penance we may be united with Christ, who was crucified for our sins, and so share with all mankind in his resurrection.**

> **Let us kneel** *(or:* **Bow your heads before God).**

All pray in silence for a brief period.

> **Let us stand** *(or:* **Raise your heads).**

> **Lord, our God and Father,**
> **through the passion of your Son**
> **you gave us new life.**
> **By our practice of penance**
> **make us one with him in his dying**
> **so that we and all mankind**
> **may be one with him**
> **in his resurrection**

> **We ask this through Christ our Lord.**
> **R.   Amen.**

Or:

Almighty and merciful Father,
send your Holy Spirit
to inspire and strengthen us,
so that by always carrying
the death of Jesus in our bodies
we may also show forth the power of his risen life.

We ask this through Christ our Lord.
R. Amen.

READINGS

16. c)

First Reading
Isaiah 53:1-7, 10:12   He is the one who bore our sufferings.

Responsorial Psalm
Psalm 22:2-3, 7-9, 18-28

Second Reading
1 Peter 2:20-25   You had gone astray but now you have
come back to the shepherd and guardian of your souls.

Gospel

Verse before the gospel
Glory to you, Lord; you were given up to death for our
sins and rose again for our justification. Glory to you,
Lord.

Or an appropriate song may be sung.

Mark 10:32-45 (or short form: *Mark 10:32-34, 42-45)*
Now we are going up to Jerusalem, and the Son of Man will
be handed over.

HOMILY

17. d)

The celebrant may speak about:

- sin, by which we offend God and also Christ's body, the Church, whose members we became in baptism;
- sin as a failure of love for Christ who in the paschal mystery showed his love for us to the end;
- the way we affect each other when we do good or choose evil;
- the mystery of vicarious satisfaction by which Christ bore the burden of our sins, so that by his wounds we would be healed (see Isaiah 53; 1 Peter 2:24);
- the social and ecclesial dimension of penance by which individual Christians share in the work of converting the whole community;
- the celebration of Easter as the feast of the Christian community which is renewing itself by the conversion or repentance of each member, so that the Church may become a clearer sign of salvation in the world.

EXAMINATION OF CONSCIENCE

18.   e)

After the homily, the examination of conscience takes place; a sample text is given in Appendix III, page 121. A period of silence should always be included so that each person may personally examine his conscience.

ACT OF REPENTANCE

19.   f)

After the examination of conscience, all say together:

> **I confess to almighty God,**
> **and to you, my brothers and sisters,**
> **that I have sinned through my own fault**

They strike their breast:

> **in my thoughts and in my words,**
> **in what I have done,**
> **and in what I have failed to do;**
> **and I ask blessed Mary, ever virgin,**
> **all the angels and saints,**
> **and you, my brothers and sisters,**
> **to pray for me to the Lord our God.**

As a sign of conversion and charity toward others, it should be suggested that the faithful give something to help the poor to celebrate the feast of Easter with joy; or they might visit the sick, or make up for some injustice in the community, or perform similar works.

Then the Lord's Prayer may be said, which the priest concludes in this way:

Deliver us, Father, from every evil
as we unite ourselves through penance
with the saving passion of your Son.
Grant us a share
in the joy of the resurrection of Jesus
who is Lord for ever and ever.

R.   Amen.

Depending on circumstances, the general confession may be followed by a form of devotion such as adoration of the cross or the way of the cross, according to local customs and the wishes of the people.

At the end, an appropriate song is sung, and the people are sent away with a greeting or blessing.

II Penitential Celebration During Advent

20.   a)   After an appropriate song and the greeting by the minister, the meaning of the celebration is explained in these or similar words:

> **My brothers and sisters, Advent is a time of preparation, when we make ready to celebrate the mystery of our Lord's coming as man, the beginning of our redemption. Advent also moves us to look forward with renewed hope to the second coming of Christ, when God's plan of salvation will be brought to fulfillment. We are reminded too of our Lord's coming to each one of us at the hour of our death. We must make sure that he will find us prepared for his coming, as the gospel tells us: "Blessed are those servants who are found awake when the Lord comes"** *(Luke 12:37).* **This service of penance is meant to make us ready in mind and heart for the coming of Christ, which we are soon to celebrate in the Mass of Christmas.**

Or:

> **Now it is time for you to wake from sleep, for our salvation is nearer to us than it was when we first believed. The night is ending; the day draws near. Let us then cast off the deeds of darkness and put on the armor of**

light. Let us live honestly as people do in the daylight, not in carousing and drunkenness, not in lust and debauchery, not in quarreling and jealousy. But rather let us put on the Lord Jesus Christ and give no thought to the desires of the flesh.

(Romans 13:11-12)

PRAYER

21.   b)

My brothers and sisters, we look forward to celebrating the mystery of Christ's coming on the feast of Christmas. Let us pray that when he comes he may find us awake and ready to receive him.

All pray in silence for a brief period.

Lord our God,
maker of the heavens,
as we look forward to the coming of our redeemer
grant us the forgiveness of our sins.

We ask this through Christ our Lord.
R. Amen.

Or:

Eternal Son of God,
creator of the human family
and our redeemer,
come at last among us
as the child of the immaculate Virgin,
and redeem the world.
Reveal your loving presence
by which you set us free from sin
in becoming one like us
in all things but sin,
for you live and reign for ever and ever.

R. Amen.

READINGS

22.   c)

First Reading
Malachi 3:1-7a   The Lord whom you seek will come to his temple.

Responsorial Psalm
Psalm 85:1-13
> R. *(8):* **Lord, let us see your kindness, and grant us your salvation.**

Second Reading
Revelation 21:1-12   He will wipe away all the tears from their eyes.

Gospel
Verse before the gospel
> **I am coming quickly, says the Lord, and I will repay each man.**
> **Come, Lord Jesus.**

Or:

> **The Spirit and the Bride say: "Come."**
> **Let all who hear answer: "Come."**
> **Come, Lord Jesus.**

Or another appropriate song may be sung.

Matthew 3:1-12   Repent, for the kingdom of heaven is close at hand.

Or:

Luke 3:3-17   All mankind shall see the salvation of God.

EXAMINATION OF CONSCIENCE

23.   d)

After the homily, the examination of conscience takes place; a sample text is given in Appendix III, page 121. A period of silence should always be included so that each person may personally examine his conscience.

ACT OF REPENTANCE

24.   e)

The act of repentance follows the examination of conscience. All may say the *I confess to almighty God* or the intercessions as in no. 60.

The Lord's Prayer is said or sung, and is concluded by the presiding minister in this way:

Lord our God,
on the first day of creation
you made the light
that scatters all darkness.
Let Christ, the light of lights,
hidden from all eternity,
shine at last on your people
and free us from the darkness of sin.
Fill our lives with good works
as we go out to meet your Son,
so that we may give him a fitting welcome.

We ask this through Christ our Lord.
R. Amen.

Or:

Almighty and eternal God,
you sent your only-begotten Son
to reconcile the world to yourself.
Lift from our hearts
the oppressive gloom of sin,
so that we may celebrate
the approaching dawn of Christ's birth
with fitting joy.

We ask this through Christ our Lord.
R. Amen.

At the end, a song is sung, and the people are sent away with a greeting or blessing.

III   Common Penitential Celebrations

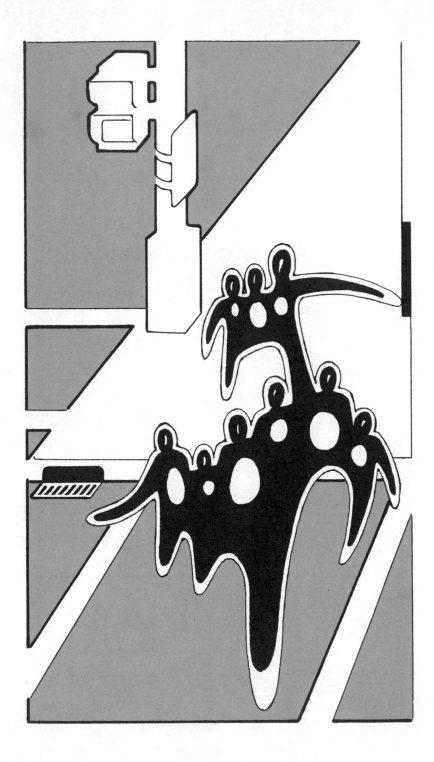

I. SIN AND CONVERSION

25.   a)

After an appropriate song (for example *Psalm 139: 1-12, 16, 23-24)* and greeting, the minister who presides briefly explains the meaning of the readings. Then he invites all to pray.

After a period of silence, he concludes the prayer in this way:

Lord Jesus,
you turned and looked on Peter
when he denied you for the third time.
He wept for his sin
and turned again to you in sincere repentance.
Look now on us and touch our hearts,
so that we also may turn back to you
and be always faithful in serving you,
for you live and reign for ever and ever.

R. Amen.

READINGS

26.   b)

First Reading
Luke 22:31-34   I tell you, Peter: the cock will not crow today before you deny me three times.

A short period of silence follows the reading.

Second Reading
Luke 22:54-62   Peter went out and wept bitterly.

Responsorial Psalm
Psalm 31:10, 15-17, 20 or *Psalm 51* or another appropriate song.

Gospel
John 21:15-19   Simon, son of John, do you love me?

HOMILY

27.   c)

The celebrant may speak about:

—the trust we must put in God's grace, not in our own powers;
—the faithfulness by which we as baptized Christians must live as true and faithful followers of the Lord;
—our weakness by which we often fall into sin and refuse to give witness to the gospel;
—the mercy of the Lord, who welcomes as a friend the one who turns to him with his whole heart.

EXAMINATION OF CONSCIENCE

28.   d)

After the homily, the examination of conscience takes place; a sample text is given in Appendix III, page 121. A period of silence should always be included so that each person may personally examine his conscience.

ACT OF REPENTANCE

29. e)

After the examination of conscience, the presiding minister invites all to prayer in these or similar words:

> **God gives us an example of love: when we were sinners he first loved us and took pity on us. Let us turn to him with a sincere heart, and in the words of Peter say to him:**
>
> **R. Lord, you know all things; you know that I love you.**

A short period of silence should follow each invocation. Each invocation may be said by different individuals, the rest answering.

> **Lord, like Peter we have relied on our own strength rather than on grace. Look on us, Lord, and have mercy.**
>
> **R. Lord, you know all things; you know that I love you.**
>
> **Our pride and foolishness have led us into temptation. Look on us, Lord, and have mercy.**
>
> **R. Lord, you know all things; you know that I love you.**
>
> **We have been vain and self-important. Look on us, Lord, and have mercy.**
>
> **R. Lord, you know all things; you know that I love you.**
>
> **We have at times been pleased rather than saddened by the misfortunes of others. Look on us, Lord, and have mercy.**
>
> **R. Lord, you know all things; you know that I love you.**
>
> **We have shown indifference for those in need instead of helping them. Look on us, Lord, and have mercy.**
>
> **R. Lord, you know all things; you know that I love you.**
>
> **We have been afraid to stand up for justice and truth. Look on us, Lord, and have mercy.**

R. Lord, you know all things; you know that I love you.

We have repeatedly broken the promises of our baptism and failed to be your disciples. Look on us, Lord, and have mercy.

R. Lord, you know all things; you know that I love you.

Let us now pray to the Father in the words Christ gave us and ask forgiveness for our sins:

Our Father . . .

30.   f)

After an appropriate song, the presiding minister says the final prayer and dismisses the people:

Lord Jesus, our Savior,
you called Peter to be an apostle;
when he repented of his sin
you restored him to your friendship
and confirmed him as first of the apostles.
Turn to us with love
and help us to imitate Peter's example.
Give us strength to turn from our sins
and to serve you in the future
with greater love and devotion,
for you live and reign for ever and ever.

R. Amen.

II. THE SON RETURNS TO THE FATHER

31. a)

After an appropriate song and the greeting by the minister, the theme of the celebration is explained to the community. Then he invites all to pray. After a period of silence, he says:

Almighty God,
you are the Father of us all.
You created the human family
to dwell for ever with you
and to praise your glory.
Open our ears to hear your voice
so that we may return to you
with sincere repentance for our sins.
Teach us to see in you our loving Father,
full of compassion for all who call to you for help.
We know that you punish us only to set us free from evil
and that you are ready to forgive us our sins.
Restore your gift of salvation
which alone brings true happiness,
so that we may all return to our Father's house
and share your table
now and for ever.

R. Amen.

READINGS

32.   b)

First Reading
Ephesians 1:3-7   He chose us from all eternity to be his adopted sons and daughters.

Responsorial Psalm
Psalm 27:1, 4, 7-10, 13-14

Gospel
Luke 15:11-32   His father saw him and was filled with pity.

HOMILY

33.   c)

The minister may speak about:

—sin as a turning away from the love we should have for God our Father;
—the limitless mercy of our Father for his children who have sinned;
—the nature of true conversion;
—the forgiveness we should extend to our brothers;
—the eucharistic banquet as the culmination of our reconciliation with the Church and with God.

EXAMINATION OF CONSCIENCE

34.   d)

After the homily, the examination of conscience takes place; a sample text is given in Appendix III, page 121. A period of silence should always be included so that each person may personally examine his conscience.

ACT OF REPENTANCE

35.   e)

After the examination of conscience, the presiding minister invites all to pray:

Our God is a God of mercy, slow to anger and full of patience. He is the father who welcomes his son when he returns from a distant country. Let us pray to him with trust in his goodness:

R. We are not worthy to be called your children.

By our misuse of your gifts we have sinned against you.

R. We are not worthy to be called your children.

By straying from you in mind and heart we have sinned against you.

R. We are not worthy to be called your children.

By forgetting your love we have sinned against you.

R. We are not worthy to be called your children.

By indulging ourselves, while neglecting our true good and the good of our neighbor, we have sinned against you.

R. We are not worthy to be called your children.

By failing to help our neighbor in his need we have sinned against you.

R. We are not worthy to be called your children.

By being slow to forgive we have sinned against you.

R. We are not worthy to be called your children.

By failing to remember your repeated forgiveness we have sinned against you.

R. We are not worthy to be called your children.

Members of the congregation may add other invocations. A brief period of silence should follow each invocation. It may be desirable to have different individuals say each invocation.

Let us now call upon our Father in the words that Jesus gave us, and ask him to forgive us our sins:

Our Father . . .

36.   f)

After an appropriate song, the presiding minister says the final prayer and dismisses the people:

God our Father,
you chose us to be your children,
to be holy in your sight
and happy in your presence.
Receive us as a loving Father
so that we may share the joy and love
of your holy Church.

We ask this through Christ our Lord.
R. Amen.

III. THE BEATITUDES

37. a)

After an appropriate song and greeting of the minister, the person presiding explains briefly the meaning of the readings. Then he invites all to pray. After a period of silence, he says:

**Lord,
open our ears and our hearts today
to the message of your Son,
so that through the power of his death and resurrection
we may walk in newness of life.**

**We ask this through Christ our Lord.
R. Amen.**

READINGS

38. b)

First Reading
1 John 1:5-9   If we say that we have no sin, we are deceiving ourselves.

Responsorial Psalm
Psalm 146:5-10

Gospel
Matthew 5:1-10   Happy are the poor in spirit, for theirs is the kingdom of heaven.

HOMILY

39.   c)

The minister may speak about:

> —sin, by which we ignore the commandments of Christ
> and act contrary to the teaching of the beatitudes;
> —the firmness of our faith in the words of Jesus;
> —our faithfulness in imitating Christ in our private lives, in
> the Christian community, and in human society;
> —each beatitude.

EXAMINATION OF CONSCIENCE

40.   d)

After the homily, the examination of conscience takes place; a sample text is given in Appendix III, page 121. A period of silence should always be included so that each person may personally examine his conscience.

ACT OF REPENTANCE

41.   e)

After the examination of conscience, the presiding minister invites all to pray in these or similar words:

> **My brothers and sisters, Jesus Christ has left an example for us to follow. Humbly and confidently let us ask him to renew us in spirit so that we may shape our lives according to the teaching of his Gospel.**

> **—Lord Jesus Christ, you said:**
> **"Blessed are the poor in spirit,**
> **for theirs is the kingdom of heaven."**
> **Yet we are preoccupied with money and worldly goods and even try to increase them at the expense of justice.**
> **Lamb of God, you take away the sin of the world:**

> **R. Have mercy on us.**

—Lord Jesus Christ, you said:
"Blessed are the gentle,
for they shall inherit the earth."
Yet we are ruthless with each other,
and our world is full of discord and violence.
Lamb of God, you take away the sin of the world:

R. Have mercy on us.

—Lord Jesus Christ, you said:
"Blessed are those who mourn,
for they shall be comforted."
Yet we are impatient under our own burdens
and unconcerned about the burdens of others.
Lamb of God, you take away the sin of the world:

R. Have mercy on us.

—Lord Jesus Christ, you said:
"Blessed are those who hunger and thirst for justice,
for they shall be filled."
Yet we do not thirst for you, the fountain of all holiness,
and are slow to spread your influence
in our private lives or in society.
Lamb of God, you take away the sin of the world:

R. Have mercy on us.

—Lord Jesus Christ, you said:
"Blessed are the merciful,
for they shall receive mercy."
Yet we are slow to forgive
and quick to condemn.
Lamb of God, you take away the sin of the world:

R. Have mercy on us.

—Lord Jesus Christ, you said:
"Blessed are the clean of heart,
for they shall see God."
Yet we are prisoners of our senses and evil desires
and dare not raise our eyes to you.
Lamb of God, you take away the sin of the world:

R. Have mercy on us.

—Lord Jesus Christ, you said:
"Blessed are the peacemakers,
for they shall be called children of God."
Yet we fail to make peace in our families,
in our country, and in the world.
Lamb of God, you take away the sin of the world:

R. Have mercy on us.

—Lord Jesus Christ, you said:
"Blessed are those who are persecuted
for the sake of justice,
for the kingdom of heaven is theirs."
Yet we prefer to practice injustice
rather than suffer for the sake of right;
we discriminate against our neighbors
and oppress and persecute them.
Lamb of God, you take away the sin of the world:

R. Have mercy on us.

—Now let us turn to God our Father and ask him to free
us from evil and prepare us for the coming of his
kingdom:

Our Father . . .

42.   f)

After an appropriate song, the presiding minister says the
final prayer and dismisses the people:

Lord Jesus Christ,
gentle and humble of heart,
full of compassion and maker of peace,
you lived in poverty
and were persecuted in the cause of justice.
You chose the cross as the path to glory
to show us the way to salvation.
May we receive with joyful hearts
the word of your Gospel
and live by your example
as heirs and citizens of your kingdom,
where you live and reign for ever and ever.

R. Amen.

IV   For Children

43.   This service is suitable for younger children, including those who have not yet participated in the sacrament of penance.

Theme: GOD COMES TO LOOK FOR US

44.   The penitential celebration should be prepared with the children so that they will understand its meaning and purpose, be familiar with the songs, have at least an elementary knowledge of the biblical text to be read, and know what they are to say and in what order.

GREETING

45.   a)

When the children have come together in the church or some other suitable place, the celebrant greets them in a friendly manner. Briefly he reminds them why they have come together and recounts the theme of the service. After the greeting, an opening song may be sung.

READING

46. b)

The celebrant may give a short introduction to the reading in these or similar words:

> **My dear children, each one of us has been baptized, and so we are all sons and daughters of God. God loves us as a Father, and he asks us to love him with all our hearts. He also wants us to be good to each other, so that we may all live happily together.**
>
> **But people do not always do what God wants. They say: "I will not obey! I am going to do as I please." They disobey God and do not want to listen to him. We, too, often act like that.**
>
> **That is what we call sin. When we sin we turn our backs on God. If we do something really bad we cut ourselves off from God; we are complete strangers to him.**
>
> **What does God do when someone turns away from him? What does he do when we leave the path of goodness that he has shown us, when we run the risk of losing the life of grace he has given us? Does God turn away from us when we turn away from him by our sins?**
>
> **Here is what God does, in the words of Jesus himself:**

47. Only one text of Scripture should be read.

Luke 15:1-7 Heaven is filled with joy when one sinner turns back to God.

HOMILY

48. c)

The homily should be short, proclaiming God's love for us and preparing the ground for the examination of conscience.

EXAMINATION OF CONSCIENCE

49. d)

The celebrant should adapt the examination to the children's level of understanding by brief comments. There should be a suitable period of silence (see Appendix III, page 121).

ACT OF REPENTANCE

50.　e)

This litany may be said by the celebrant or by one or more of the children, alternating with all present. Before the response, which may be sung, all should observe a brief pause.

God our Father,

—Sometimes we have not behaved as your children should.

　　R. But you love us and come to us.

—We have given trouble to our parents and teachers.

　　R. But you love us and come to us.

—We have quarrelled and called each other names.

　　R. But you love us and come to us.

—We have been lazy at home and in school, and have not been helpful to our parents (brothers, sisters, friends).

　　R. But you love us and come to us.

—We have thought too much of ourselves and have told lies.

　　R. But you love us and come to us.

—We have not done good to others when we had the chance.

　　R. But you love us and come to us.

Now with Jesus, our brother, we come before our Father in heaven and ask him to forgive our sins:

Our Father . . .

ACT OF CONTRITION AND PURPOSE OF AMENDMENT
51.   f)

Sorrow may be shown by some sign, for example, individual children may come to the altar or another suitable place with a candle, and light it there; if necessary, a server may help. Each child says in his own words:

> **Father,**
> **I am sorry for all my sins:**
> **for what I have done**
> **and for what I have failed to do.**
> **I will sincerely try to do better**
> **especially . . . (he mentions his particular resolution).**
> **Help me to walk by your light.**

In place of the candle, or in addition to it, the children may prepare a written prayer or resolution and place it on the altar or on a table designated for this purpose.

If the number of children or other circumstances do not allow for this, the celebrant asks the children present to say the above prayer together, along with a general resolution.

PRAYER OF THE CELEBRANT
52.   g)

> **God our Father always seeks us out**
> **when we walk away from the path of goodness.**
> **He is always ready to forgive**
> **when we have sinned.**
> **May almighty God have mercy on us,**
> **forgive us our sins,**
> **and bring us to everlasting life.**

> **R. Amen.**

53.   The minister invites the children to express their thanks to God. They may do this by an appropriate hymn.

Then he dismisses them.

V For Young People

54.   The penitential celebration should be prepared with the young people so that with the celebrant, they may choose or compose the texts and songs. The readers, cantors or choir should be chosen from among them.

Theme: RENEWAL OF OUR LIVES ACCORDING TO THE CHRISTIAN VOCATION

GREETING

55.   a)

This may be given in these or similar words:

> **Dear friends, we have come here to do penance and to make a fresh start as Christians. Many people see In penance only its difficult side, and its emphasis on sorrow. But it has also a more joyful side, and it looks more to the future than to the past.**
>
> **Through penance God calls us to a new beginning. He helps us to find our true freedom as his sons and daughters. When Jesus invites us to repentance, he is inviting us to take our place in his Father's kingdom. This is what he teaches us in the parable about the merchant who came across a pearl of great value and sold everything he had in order to buy it.**
>
> **If we follow our Lord's advice we exchange our past life for one far more valuable.**

Then a song is sung; it should stress the call to a new life or following God's call with an eager heart (for example, *Psalm 40:1-9   R. Here am I, Lord; I come to do your will).*

PRAYER

56.   b)

> **Lord our God,**
> **you call us out of darkness into light,**
> **out of self-deception into truth,**
> **out of death into life.**
> **Send us your Holy Spirit**
> **to open our ears to your call.**
> **Fill our hearts with courage**
> **to be true followers of your Son.**
>
> **We ask this through Christ our Lord.**
> **R. Amen.**

READINGS

57.   c)

First Reading
Romans 7:18-25   Unhappy man am I! Who will free me? Thanks to God through Jesus Christ our Lord.

Or:

Romans 8:19-23   We know that by turning everything to their good, God cooperates with all those who love him.

A song is sung, or a brief period of silence is observed.

Gospel
Matthew 13:44-46   He sold all that he had and bought the field.

HOMILY

58.   d)

The celebrant may speak about:

— the law of sin which in us struggles against God;
— the necessity of giving up the way of sin so that we may enter the kingdom of God.

EXAMINATION OF CONSCIENCE

59.　e)

After the homily, the examination of conscience takes place; a sample text is given in Appendix III, page 121. A period of silence should always be included so that each person may personally examine his conscience.

ACT OF REPENTANCE

60.　f)

Christ our Lord came to call sinners into his Father's kingdom. Let us now make an act of sorrow in our hearts and resolve to avoid sin in the future.

After a brief period of silence, all say together:

**I confess to almighty God,
and to you, my brothers and sisters,
that I have sinned through my own fault**

They strike their breast:

**in my thoughts and in my words,
in what I have done,
and in what I have failed to do;
and I ask blessed Mary, ever virgin,
all the angels and saints,
and you, my brothers and sisters,
to pray for me to the Lord our God.**

Minister:

**Lord our God,
you know all things.
You know that we want to be more generous
in serving you and our neighbor.
Look on us with love and hear our prayer.**

Reader:

Give us the strength to turn away from sin.

R. Hear our prayer.

Help us to be sorry for our sins and to keep our resolutions.

R. Hear our prayer.

Forgive our sins and have pity on our weakness.

R. Hear our prayer.

Give us trust in your goodness and make us generous in serving you.

R. Hear our prayer.

Help us to be true followers of your Son and living members of his Church.

Minister:

God does not want the sinner to die, but to turn to him and live. May he be pleased that we have confessed our sinfulness, and may he show us his great mercy as we pray in obedience to his Son.

All say together:

Our Father . . .

61.   The celebration ends with an appropriate song and the dismissal.

VI   For the Sick

62.   According to the condition of the sick people and the suitability of the place, the minister goes to the sick, gathered in one room, or else he brings them together in the sanctuary or church. He should adapt carefully the texts and their number to the condition of those who take part in the service. Since in most instances none of the sick will be able to act as reader, the minister should, if possible, invite another person to carry out this office.

Theme: **THE TIME OF SICKNESS IS A TIME OF GRACE**

GREETING

63.   a)

He may greet them in these or similar words:

> **My dear friends, when Jesus came to preach repentance, he was bringing us good news, for he was proclaiming to us God's love and mercy. Again and again God comes to our help so that we may turn to him and live our lives entirely in his service. Penance is his gift, a gift we should accept with gratitude. Keeping this in mind, let us open our hearts to God with great simplicity and humility and ask to be reconciled with him as we now forgive each other.**

If possible, a penitential song is sung by the sick persons, or by a choir.

PRAYER

64. b)

Lord our God,
source of all goodness and mercy,
we come together as your family
to ask your forgiveness
and the forgiveness of each other.
Give us true sorrow for our sins
and loving trust in your compassion
so that we may acknowledge our sins
with sincere hearts.
Through this celebration
restore us to fuller union with yourself
and with our neighbor
so that we may serve you with greater generosity.

We ask this through Christ our Lord.
R. Amen.

READINGS

65. c)

The readings may be introduced in these or similar words:

Many people enjoy good health and other blessings and accept them as a matter of course, with no sense of gratitude. In time of sickness we discover that all these are great gifts, and that without them we easily lose heart. God allows us to experience sickness in order to test our faith. What is more, if we see our suffering as a share in Christ's suffering, it can be of great value both to ourselves and to the Church. The time of sickness is not then wasted or meaningless. It is in fact a time of grace if we accept it as God wants us to accept it. This celebration is meant to help us to do so. We shall therefore listen to God's word, examine our conscience, and pray with sincere hearts.

66.   First Reading
James 5:13-16   The prayer of faith will save the sick man.

Responsorial Psalm
Between the readings, a psalm may be said or sung alternately, for example, *Psalm 130* or *Psalm 51*.

Gospel
Mark 2:1-12   The Son of Man has authority on earth to forgive sins.

HOMILY

67.   d)

It is fitting that the celebrant speak of sickness, dwelling not so much on sickness of the body as on sickness of the soul. He should emphasize the power of Jesus and his Church to forgive sins and the value of suffering offered for others.

EXAMINATION OF CONSCIENCE

68.   e)

After the homily, the examination of conscience takes place; a sample text is given in Appendix III, page 121. A period of silence should always be included so that each person may personally examine his conscience.

The following questions may be added but adapted to the condition of the sick:

—**Do I trust God's goodness and providence, even in times of stress and illness?**

—**Do I give in to sickness, to despair, to other unworthy thoughts and feelings?**

—**Do I fill my empty moments with reflection on life and with prayer to God?**

—**Do I accept my illness and pain as an opportunity for suffering with Christ, who redeemed us by his passion?**

—**Do I live by faith, confident that patience in suffering is of great benefit to the Church?**

—Am I thoughtful of others and attentive to my fellow patients and their needs?

—Am I grateful to those who look after me and visit me?

—Do I give a good Christian example to others?

—Am I sorry for my past sins, and do I try to make amends for them by my patient acceptance of weakness and illness?

ACT OF REPENTANCE

69.   f)

After a moment of silence, all say together:

> I confess to almighty God,
> and to you, my brothers and sisters,
> that I have sinned through my own fault

They strike their breast:

> in my thoughts and in my words,
> in what I have done,
> and in what I have failed to do;
> and I ask blessed Mary, ever virgin,
> all the angels and saints,
> and you, my brothers and sisters,
> to pray for me to the Lord our God.

Reader:

> Lord our God, we bear the name of your Son and call you Father. We are sorry for our sins against you and against our brothers and sisters.
>
> R. Give us true repentance and sincere love for you and for our neighbor.
>
> Lord Jesus Christ, you redeemed us by your passion and cross and gave us an example of patience and love. We are sorry for our sins against you, and especially for failing to serve you and our brothers and sisters.

R. Give us true repentance and sincere love for you and for our neighbor.

Holy Spirit, Lord, you speak to us in the Church and in our conscience and inspire within us the desire to do good. We are sorry for our sins against you, and especially for our obstinate refusal to obey you.

R. Give us true repentance and sincere love for you and for our neighbor.

Minister:

Let us ask God our Father to forgive us and to free us from evil:

Our Father . . .

70.   Then, if possible, the choir or the assembled people sing a song, and the service concludes with a prayer of thanksgiving:

71.

**God of consolation and Father of mercies,
you forgive the sinner who acknowledges his guilt:**

R. We praise you and thank you.

**God of consolation and Father of mercies,
you give to those who suffer hardship or pain
a share in the sufferings of your Son
for the salvation of the world:**

R. We praise you and thank you.
**God of consolation and Father of mercies,
you look with love on those who are troubled or in sorrow;
you give them hope of salvation
and the promise of eternal life:**

R. We praise you and thank you.

117

Let us pray.

Lord,
your goodness and mercy are boundless.
Look on your sons and daughters
gathered here in the name of your Son.
We thank you for all your gifts
and ask you to keep us always as your family,
full of living faith, firm hope,
and sincere love for you and for our neighbor.

We ask this through Christ our Lord.
R. Amen.

72.   In place of the prayer, the service may end with a
blessing.

May the God of peace
fill your hearts with every blessing.
May he sustain you
with his gifts of hope and consolation,
help you to offer your lives in his service,
and bring you safely to eternal glory.
May almighty God,
the Father, and the Son, ☩ and the Holy Spirit,
grant you all that is good.

R. Amen.

73.   The minister dismisses the assembly, or invites those
present to a friendly visit with the sick.

Part Three

---•◆•---

Form of
Examination of Conscience

Appendix III, Rite of Penance

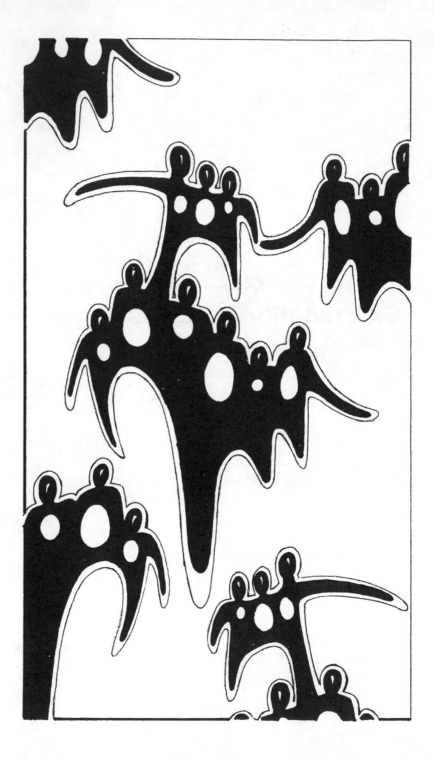

EXAMINATION OF CONSCIENCE

1. This suggested form for an examination of conscience should be completed and adapted to meet the needs of different individuals and to follow local usages.

2. In an examination of conscience, before the sacrament of penance, each individual should ask himself these questions in particular:

1. What is my attitude to the sacrament of penance? Do I sincerely want to be set free from sin, to turn again to God, to begin a new life, and to enter into a deeper friendship with God? Or do I look on it as a burden, to be undertaken as seldom as possible?

2. Did I forget to mention, or deliberately conceal, any grave sins in past confessions?

3. Did I perform the penance I was given? Did I make reparation for any injury to others? Have I tried to put into practice my resolution to lead a better life in keeping with the Gospel?

3. Each individual should examine his life in the light of God's word.

I. The Lord says: "You shall love the Lord your God with your whole heart."

1.   Is my heart set on God, so that I really love him above all things and am faithful to his commandments, as a son loves his father? Or am I more concerned about the things of this world? Have I a right intention in what I do?

2.   God spoke to us in his Son. Is my faith in God firm and secure? Am I wholehearted in accepting the Church's teaching? Have I been careful to grow in my understanding of the faith, to hear God's word, to listen to instructions on the faith, to avoid dangers to faith? Have I been always strong and fearless in professing my faith in God and the Church? Have I been willing to be known as a Christian in private and public life?

3.   Have I prayed morning and evening? When I pray, do I really raise my mind and heart to God or is it a matter of words only? Do I offer God my difficulties, my joys, and my sorrows? Do I turn to God in time of temptation?

4.   Have I love and reverence for God's name? Have I offended him in blasphemy, swearing falsely, or taking his name in vain? Have I shown disrespect for the Blessed Virgin Mary and the saints?

5.   Do I keep Sundays and feast days holy by taking a full part, with attention and devotion, in the liturgy, and especially in the Mass? Have I fulfilled the precept of annual confession and of communion during the Easter season?

6.   Are there false gods that I worship by giving them greater attention and deeper trust than I give to God: money, superstition, spiritism, or other occult practices?

II. The Lords says: "Love one another as I have loved you."

1.   Have I a genuine love for my neighbors? Or do I use them for my own ends, or do to them what I would not want done to myself? Have I given grave scandal by my words or actions?

2.   In my family life, have I contributed to the well-being and happiness of the rest of the family by patience and genuine love? Have I been obedient to parents, showing them proper respect and giving them help in their spiritual and material needs? Have I been careful to give a Christian upbringing to my children, and to help them by good example and by exercising authority as a parent. Have I been faithful to my husband (wife) in my heart and in my relations with others?

3.   Do I share my possessions with the less fortunate? Do I do my best to help the victims of oppression, misfortune, and poverty? Or do I look down on my neighbor, especially the poor, the sick, the elderly, strangers, and people of other races?

4.   Does my life reflect the mission I received in confirmation? Do I share in the apostolic and charitable works of the Church and in the life of my parish? Have I helped to meet the needs of the Church and of the world and prayed for them: for unity in the Church, for the spread of the Gospel among the nations, for peace and justice, etc.?

5.   Am I concerned for the good and prosperity of the human community in which I live, or do I spend my life caring only for myself? Do I share to the best of my ability in the work of promoting justice, morality, harmony, and love in human relations? Have I done my duty as a citizen? Have I paid my taxes?

6. In my work or profession am I just, hard-working, honest, serving society out of love for others? Have I paid a fair wage to my employees? Have I been faithful to my promises and contracts?

7. Have I obeyed legitimate authority and given it due respect?

8. If I am in a position of responsibility or authority, do I use this for my own advantage or for the good of others, in a spirit of service?

9. Have I been truthful and fair, or have I injured others by deceit, calumny, detraction, rash judgment, or violation of a secret?

10. Have I done violence to others by damage to life or limb, reputation, honor, or material possessions? Have I involved them in loss? Have I been responsible for advising an abortion or procuring one? Have I kept up hatred for others? Am I estranged from others through quarrels, enmity, insults, anger? Have I been guilty of refusing to testify to the innocence of another because of selfishness?

11. Have I stolen the property of others? Have I desired it unjustly and inordinately? Have I damaged it? Have I made restitution of other people's property and made good their loss?

12. If I have been injured, have I been ready to make peace for the love of Christ and to forgive, or do I harbor hatred and the desire for revenge?

III. Christ our Lord says: "Be perfect as your Father is perfect."

1. Where is my life really leading me? Is the hope of eternal life my inspiration? Have I tried to grow in the life of the Spirit through prayer, reading the word of God and meditating on it, receiving the sacraments, self-denial? Have I been anxious to control my vices, my bad inclinations and passions, e.g., envy, love of food and drink? Have I been proud and boastful, thinking myself better in the sight of God and despising others as less important than myself? Have I imposed my own will on others, without respecting their freedom and rights?

2. What use have I made of time, of health and strength, of the gifts God has given me to be used like the talents in the Gospel? Do I use them to become more perfect every day? Or have I been lazy and too much given to leisure?

3. Have I been patient in accepting the sorrows and disappointments of life? How have I performed mortification so as to "fill up what is wanting to the sufferings of Christ"? Have I kept the precept of fasting and abstinence?

4. Have I kept my senses and my whole body pure and chaste as a temple of the Holy Spirit consecrated for resurrection and glory, and as a sign of God's faithful love for men and women, a sign that is seen most perfectly in the sacrament of matrimony? Have I dishonored my body by fornication, impurity, unworthy conversation or thoughts, evil desires, or actions? Have I given in to sensuality? Have I indulged in reading, conversation, shows, and entertainments that offend against Christian and human decency? Have I

encouraged others to sin by my own failure to maintain these standards? Have I been faithful to the moral law in my married life?

5.   Have I gone against my conscience out of fear or hypocrisy?

6.   Have I always tried to act in the true freedom of the sons of God according to the law of the Spirit, or am I the slave of forces within me?

Song References

1. "On Jordan's Bank," John Chandler, *Catholic Liturgy Book*, Helicon Press; *People's Mass Book*, World Library Publications; *Worship*, G.I.A. Publications

2. "O Come, O Come, Emmanuel," John Neale, *Catholic Liturgy Book*, Helicon Press; *People's Mass Book*, World Library Publications; *Worship*, G.I.A. Publications

3. "O Come, All Ye Faithful," traditional, *Catholic Liturgy Book*, Helicon Press; *People's Mass Book*, World Library Publications, *Worship*, G.I.A. Publications

4. "Like Olive Branches," Lucien Deiss, *Young People's Folk Hymnal I*, World Library Publications

5. "I Will Celebrate Your Love Forever, Yahweh (Psalm 89)," Karen Barrie, 4643 N. Central Park, Chicago, 60625

6. "Draw Near, O Lord Our God," Melvin Farrell, *Catholic Liturgy Book*, Helicon Press; *People's Mass Book*, World Library Publications; *Worship*, G.I.A. Publications

7. "Now Thank We All Our God," C. Winkworth, *People's Mass Book*, World Library Publications; *Worship*, G.I.A. Publications

8. "Come, Holy Ghost," traditional, *People's Mass Book*, World Library Publications; *Worship*, G.I.A. Publications

9. "The Spirit Is A'Movin'," Carey Landry, *Hi God Music Book*, North American Liturgy Resources

10. "Veni Creator Spiritus," traditional, *Catholic Liturgy Book*, Helicon Press; *People's Mass Book*, Voice Book, World Library Publications; *Worship*, G.I.A. Publications

11. "Bring to the Lord," Jack Miffleton, The American Catholic Press

12. "Peace I Leave With You" (Peace Song), Judy O'Sheil, F.E.L. Publications

13. "Here We Are," Ray Repp, F.E.L. Publications

14. "Be a New Man," Joe Wise, *Young People's Folk Hymnal II*, World Library Publications

15. "God Has Visited His People," James Haas, *Rainbow Songs*, Morehouse-Barlow

16. "I'm Ready to Follow," Jack Miffleton, *With Skins and Steel*, World Library Publications

17. Telespots, Teleketics, Franciscan Communications
18. "Where Charity and Love Prevail," traditional, *People's Mass Book,* World Library Publications
19. "I Must Remember," Lou Fortunate, *God Among Us,* William H. Sadlier, Inc.
20. "I Will Not Forget You," Carey Landry, North American Liturgy Resources
21. "Care Is All It Takes," Jack Miffleton, *Even a Worm,* World Library Publications
22. "Lord, Who at Thy First Eucharist," *People's Mass Book,* World Library Publications
23. "Pange Lingua," traditional, *Catholic Liturgy Book,* Helicon Press; *People's Mass Book,* World Library Publications
24. "Sing, My Tongue, the Savior's Glory," traditional, *Worship,* G.I.A. Publications
25. "Father, We Thank Thee," F. Bland Tucker, *Catholic Liturgy Book,* Helicon Press; *People's Mass Book,* World Library Publications; *Worship,* G.I.A. Publications

Addresses for References

The American Catholic Press
1223 N. Rossell Avenue
Oak Park, IL 60302

Karen Barrie
4643 N. Central Park
Chicago, IL 60625

F.E.L. Publications
1925 Pontius Avenue
Los Angeles, CA 90025

G.I.A. Publications, Inc.
7404 S. Mason Avenue
Chicago, IL 60638

Helicon Press
1120 N. Calvert Street
Baltimore, MD 21202

Morehouse-Barlow Co.
78 Danbury Road
Wilton, Conn. 06897

North American Liturgy Resources
300 E. McMillan Street
Cincinnati, OH 45219

William H. Sadlier, Inc.
11 Park Place
New York, NY 10007

Teleketics
Franciscan Communications
1229 South Santee Street
Los Angeles, CA 90015

World Library Publications
2145 Central Parkway
Cincinnati, OH 45214